Peter Schreiner

The Creative Dribbler

Library of Congress Cataloging - in - Publication Data

Schreiner, Peter
  The Creative Dribbler

ISBN Number 1-890946028-1
Library of Congress Catalog Card Number 99-074798
Copyright © August 1999

Originally Published in Germany 1999

Art Direction and Layout
Kimberly N. Bender

Editing and Proofing
Bryan R. Beaver

Photography
Hans Wittkowski

Printed by
DATA REPRODUCTIONS
Auburn Hills, Michigan

REEDSWAIN INC
612 Pughtown Road
Spring City, Pennsylvania 19475
1-800-331-5191
www.reedswain.com

Peter Schreiner

The Creative Dribbler

published by
REEDSWAIN INC

FOREWORD

I have known Peter Schreiner since 1990, when we crossed swords as rival coaches in a German regional league. I am pleased that Peter Schreiner the author has turned to junior soccer and has drawn on his wide and rich experience to write this book, in which he presents his ideas on how best to coach youngsters in the basic techniques of soccer.

I have been privileged to attend a number of demonstration sessions in which Peter Schreiner presented and explained his coaching method with the help of junior players of the famous German club, FC Schalke 04. These demonstrations and explanations impressed not only me but also the knowledgeable coaches who were present.

The strong point of the Peter-Schreiner-System, in my opinion, is that children learn typical soccer movements systematically in the course of a dynamic learning process. The coaching is intensive, varied and, above all, child-oriented.

New stimulating organizational frameworks (circuits) help the players to steadily improve their ball control and touch. One of Peter Schreiner's major achievements is that he describes the basic movements, circuits and feints exactly and comprehensibly.

The subject of junior soccer is attracting a lot of public attention. The book "The Creative Dribbler" contains many fundamental ideas about the coaching of our young soccer players. Coaches and teachers will find many exciting suggestions for effective and varied training sessions.

I admire Peter Schreiner's dedication to encouraging junior soccer and I wish him and his book every success.

I hope that all soccer-loving readers will enjoy learning about the Peter-Schreiner-System and putting it into practice.

Erich Rutemöller
(German Soccer Association coach)

Contents

Author's foreword

1986 World Cup in Mexico

In the quarter-final game between England and Argentina, Diego Maradonna made the score 2-0 after a fabulous dribble that started in his own half of the pitch. One opponent after the other was left floundering before he finished off his brilliant solo run by sliding the ball into the net. No one who saw this "goal of the century" will ever forget it.

Similar feelings are experienced by all soccer fans who have been privileged to watch soccer greats such as Péle, Cruyff or Beckenbauer in action. Ball artists of this caliber exert a fascination that will always attract huge crowds into our soccer stadiums. Soccer fans want their club and national teams to be successful, but they also want success to go hand in hand with creative, attractive play and spectacular moments of individual skill.

Soccer coaches should always be aware of this and should realize that there is more to the game than the result. They might then be able to contribute to the development of exceptionally talented young players in their own clubs.

A guide for coaches

I have written this book as a guide for all coaches(1) who work with young soccer players without having any special qualifications.

At many seminars and soccer schools in Germany I have found that many of the coaches, especially those who work with younger children, are volunteers who have taken on the job out of loyalty to their children or the club.

These coaches often feel that they are not up to the task of organizing correctly structured and effective training sessions. Nevertheless, they are enthusiastic and they try hard to teach youngsters as well as they can. I hope that this book will serve as a guide to these coaches and help them to systematically and selectively teach their charges the skills of dribbling.

Drills for children, juniors and adults

All of the drills are suitable for young players. In addition, I have found that amateur players at all levels also enjoy them. These older players can use the drills to refresh skills that they have already learned, or to eliminate weaknesses.

---

(1) The term "coaches" refers to all those, including teachers, whether male or female, who help youngsters to develop their soccer skills. Similarly, the term "player" refers to both male and female players.

Homework for the players

The contents of this book are easy to understand and are illustrated with lots of photos. Children and juniors can therefore use it as a guide for practicing on their own. They can be asked to carry out soccer homework in the periods between club training sessions. In my experience they enjoy this much more than their usual school homework, and are keen to master the basic movements that they have learned before they attend the next training session. Through carrying out the drills, the players soon acquire good ball control skills; they can dribble and run confidently with the ball under close control, can trick an opponent with any of a wide range of feints and, best of all, can play attractive and successful soccer.

Work manual with a comprehensive list of the contents

The drills are systematically described and easy to carry out. A coach can therefore use it as a work manual. This is why the list of contents is so detailed. It enables the subjects treated to be found very quickly. Most coaches want tried and tested drills, methodical tips and comprehensible instructions and descriptions. This is exactly what they will find in this book.

More than 300 photos show the sequences of movements very clearly. The Peter-Schreiner-System® can be quickly put into practice without reading the theoretical information on dribbling.

It is thus not necessary for you to read this book from front to back, page by page. Just look for the sections or photo sequences that interest you most, and work through them first. At a later stage, however, you should certainly look into the background information and methodical tips.

You should practice the described and illustrated techniques yourself before you introduce them into your training sessions. Simple things such as the correct positioning of the cones for special circuits such as the Comb or the Figure-8 are especially important and should be thought through and practiced beforehand.

Choosing the correct distance between individual cones and the correct angles between lines of cones requires a certain amount of experience. However, if you experiment with distances between 5 and 10 yards you will soon find out which ones suit your players best. As time goes by, you will also become familiar with the angles in the various circuits.

Motivation

I would be proud if I could motivate you to introduce the first drills during your next training session, even if you do not have the time to familiarize yourself perfectly with them. You would not regret it. If you use the Peter-Schreiner-System (P-S-S) selectively, your players will demonstrate techniques - also during matches - that you would never have thought them capable of.   They will eagerly practice the new techniques and will soon be able to dribble confidently round the different circuits.

If you become a skilled "disciple" of the Peter-Schreiner-System, other coaches will approach you and ask about your coaching concept.

You will be able to explain to them about the Comb, the scissor (inside-inside) and directional dribbling.

If this book makes a contribution, however small, to promoting more varied and systematic development of new generations of young soccer players, then I will be satisfied. All other age groups can also profit from the P-S-S, of course, and are welcome to try it.

Peter Schreiner

The development of the Peter-Schreiner-System (P-S-S)

No one wakes up one morning and thinks, "Today I will devise a new coaching method." Only after a long development process does an initially insignificant idea acquire a life of its own. A study of the existing literature, single-mindedness and continuous experimentation are needed to continuously develop and improve an idea.

At the age of 23 I started my career as a player-coach in a German regional league after having played for 4 years in the highest and second-highest amateur leagues. This was a big challenge for a young sports student whose ambition was to be a coach in the highest amateur league.

In 1988, at the age of 35, I achieved my ambition. The club under my charge, Sportfreunde Katernberg (Essen), for which the famous German international, Helmut Rahn, once played, was promoted to the highest amateur league.

Then, in December 1989, I received a phone call that would completely change my life as a coach and teacher. Bodo Menze, the youth development manager of one of Germany's most famous professional clubs, Schalke 04, Gelsenkirchen, asked me to coach the club's A-Juniors from the 1990/91 season onward. This was my transition from senior soccer, with which I had been enthusiastically involved for 13 years, to junior soccer, with completely new perspectives and ambitions.

After two very successful years in the amateur league, I found myself at a turning point, facing the challenge of Schalke 04 and junior soccer. I was extremely fortunate, and I am still grateful to Bodo Menze for giving me the opportunity to experience the last 8 wonderful years.

Since 1992 I have no longer been responsible for a team but have been occupied with restructuring the organization of Schalke's youth development section, from beginners to C-Juniors.

I have attended numerous courses to extend my knowledge. I have widened my horizons by acquiring licenses in the fields of refereeing and organization, and I have intensively studied the international literature on the subject of junior soccer.

During this period I came into contact with Wiel Coerver. I spent many hours learning to understand and put into practice the drills devised by this talented soccer coach.

The basic training sessions of Schalke 04 proved to be an excellent environment for experimenting, and I gradually developed my own concept. Word got around that the youngsters learned a lot during the basic coaching sessions and also enjoyed themselves. The first spectators came, as did the first inquiries. That was the time when I provided a steadily growing number of coaches with my sketches.

In 1994, despite initial difficulties and problems, Bodo Menze and I started a youth project with the name "Talentmodell Schalke 04." As project manager, my task was to organize basic training sessions, provide coaches and teachers with ideas for child-oriented and varied training sessions, and promote cooperation between the club and schools.

This new field of activity gave me the opportunity to develop creative ideas and devise a new coaching concept that would become known beyond the boundaries of Gelsenkirchen.

In 1996 I was invited to present material from the basic "Successful Dribbling" program at the International Congress of Coaches of the Federation of German Soccer Teachers in Munich. Youngsters from Schalke's E- and D-Junior teams demonstrated the effectiveness of selective coaching in dribbling techniques to more than 1000 coaches.

The response to this demonstration was overwhelming. It resulted in an invitation to the 1997 Coaches Congress in Cologne, where we had the opportunity to present more aspects of Schalke's basic coaching program. The soccer schools that I organized for FC Schalke 04 were so popular that I decided to demonstrate the Peter-Schreiner-System in soccer schools outside the auspices of Schalke.

In 1996 I founded the Institute for Youth Soccer ("Institut für Jugendfussball" - IFJ for short), with the objective of encouraging soccer for youngsters. My home page on the worldwide web (http://www.ifj.de)

serves as a platform for a stimulating exchange of ideas with youth coaches throughout the world.

Seminars for coaches were held as part of the "Talentmodell Schalke 04" project. As organizer and speaker, I presented my ideas on youth-oriented coaching. All of the participants had the opportunity to absorb ideas on the theory and practice of varied and stimulating youth coaching.

I subsequently received invitations from other clubs to organize such seminars for their own coaches. I found these to be an excellent personal forum and learning environment.

Requests from many coaches for the content of these seminars to be made available in a form that they could take home with them finally led to the production of two videotapes, which soon proved to be best-sellers.

My thanks are due to Jörg Göppel, who not only put forward the idea for the videos but also helped considerably in putting the idea into practice.

The videos also sold very well in the USA under the title "The German Touch."

During the Coaches Congress in Cincinnati in 1998, the publisher and distributor of the American videos asked me to make the contents of the videos available in book form. Many coaches had expressed interest and there was considerable demand for such a book. That was the first step. Hanjo Beese, who has been a friend of mine for many years and is also a fan of my coaching method, contacted the German publisher, Rowohlt Verlag, and thus played a considerable role in ensuring the publication of this work.

Last but not least, I would like to thank **Peter Hyballa**, who has been an invaluable discussion partner and who followed developments in this field in the press, thus enabling me to include the latest ideas.

My thanks are also due to all those who have contributed to the Peter-Schreiner-System through their encouragement, suggestions and praise.

A disciple
(Peter Hyballa)

You are a qualified youth coach. You feel that your training sessions are not always sufficiently varied. You are looking for new ways of arousing the enthusiasm of your players. This was the situation in which I found myself when I made the acquaintance of a passionate soccer "guru" called Peter Schreiner.

On a gray December morning, I, like all of the other participants at a German Soccer Association course for coaches, received a letter from the IFJ. At first glance it seemed to be nothing special. A second glance revealed, however, that IFJ stood for Institut für Jugendfussball (Institute for Youth Soccer). I was amazed and surprised that such an institute existed.

Although I am an absolutely dedicated youth coach, I had never heard of this institute. When I opened the envelope I saw references to coaching seminars and a Soccer School video on Playing With An Opponent At Your Back. I spontaneously dialed the telephone number and found myself speaking to a certain Peter Schreiner. After a short but intensive discussion about youth soccer, he suggested that I should help with a soccer school held under the name "Successful dribbling." I gladly accepted this opportunity of learning about a new coaching method first hand.

A few months later I stood alongside Peter Schreiner on the green turf of a soccer school with more than 80 children, who proceeded to go through the Zig-zag, the Comb or the Thunderbolt using a dummy step, a scissor (inside-inside) or a rotation (outside).

The soccer-mad boys and girls mastered these technically demanding circuits with gusto and, above all, with an expression in their eyes that clearly revealed their total enjoyment.

Moreover, this expression could also be seen in my own eyes.

I felt a deep sense of satisfaction, because I had learned about a new coaching method that would bring a new dimension to my own training sessions.

Peter Schreiner's idea of a systematic soccer education, in which technique, and especially dribbling, are central, rather than repetitive conditioning exercises, has retained its fascination for me since that time, because coaches are often at a loss when they have to cope with large groups. The planning and implementation of the "Successful Dribbling" coaching concept allows every player to be individually schooled, while the youth coach has every player in his field of vision and can therefore intervene to correct errors or provide encouragement.

The Peter-Schreiner-System creates the basic conditions for acquiring good ball control skills, creative attacking techniques, the ability to dribble successfully, and numerous tricks.

The method appealed to me immediately, but that alone was not enough. A coaching method also has to be put smoothly and systematically into practice. I therefore bought the videos on "Consolidating Individual Skills and Ball Control" and "Playing with an Opponent at Your Back," which I viewed very attentively. In addition I learned about motivational coordination exercises as supplementary training.

Now I could study this method in my own living room while drinking coke and eating potato chips.

After I had watched the videos several times and jotted down a lot of notes, I had a comprehensive coaching concept for my youth team.
From that time onward, keywords such as "rotation" and "drag behind the standing leg," together with numerous types of circuits, were a permanent fixture in my notebook, which I initially made frequent use of during many training sessions.

This coaching system, the associated publications and, above all, the numerous vacation soccer schools for children and young people have retained their hold on me, and I remain as enthusiastic as ever.

I became a freelance helper at the Institute for Youth Soccer and am a member of its group of coaches, some of whom work for German professional clubs while others are excellently qualified people such as teachers and sports students.

Before being admitted to this group, I attended a seminar on a rainy Saturday morning in Essen, where Peter Schreiner explained his method in clear and plausible terms, in an informal atmosphere, to the participating youth coaches.

Those of us who had expected a boring lecture based largely on theory were soon disabused. The focus was on practical aspects and the coaches had to repeatedly use and demonstrate the "dummy step (outside-outside)" or the "change of direction (outside)." All of us were soon bathed in perspiration. At the same time, however, we improved our own technique and gained the self-confidence needed to demonstrate these unusual movements to our players during training sessions.

Today I am a coach who frequently asks his plays to "dribble successfully."
When the players see me set up the cones for the Zig-zag or the Comb, I notice a certain amount of tension in the air.

The players have not yet mastered all of the tricks and are nervous or even anxious about whether they will be able to carry out, for example, the scissor (inside-inside) this time. At the same time the players are pleased to have the opportunity to dribble round the circuits, because they have already mastered many of the techniques and these become more automatic each time they are practiced.

Naturally many players are proud that they can perform some of the techniques almost automatically and are glad of the opportunity to demonstrate this again to their coach.

My colleagues in the coaching world observe my players' dribbling drills closely and are surprised that a coach can provide so much enjoyment, fun and enthusiasm with so few coaching aids (just a few cones as markers) allied to new types of circuits and interesting techniques.

I became infected by the Peter-Schreiner-System virus a long time ago. His drills have become an important part of my training sessions and I still look forward to every soccer school organized by the IFJ.

The Peter-Schreiner-System (P-S-S)

The various circuits used for training sessions involving large groups of players (see pp. 98-131) are at the heart of the P-S-S. The players dribble round a closed circuit, and as they do so they either perform a number of set tasks (see section "Basic Movements") or can carry out movements and sequences at will. The following chart shows the characteristics and key principles of the Peter-Schreiner-System. These are the platform on which his success in teaching dribbling techniques, feints and ball control skills are based. The effectiveness of the learning process with the P-S-S is in large measure due to the fact that each player is always in motion with the ball and carrying out a specific task. None of the players has to simply stand and watch.

Characteristics of the Peter-Schreiner-System

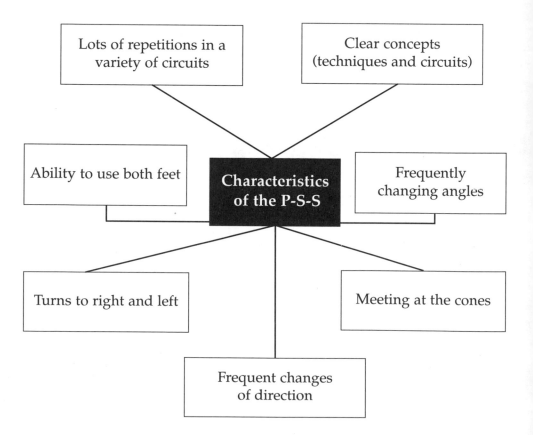

Characteristics of the P-S-S

• Lots of repetitions in a variety of circuits

When a player has learned to feint in a slow and controlled manner, he should practice this in different circuits while carrying out various tasks. The coach should therefore have a large number of different drills available, so that he can always confront his players with new challenges and they can practice the basic movements frequently and variably until they have mastered them.

In the sport of tennis, even professionals practice simple shots repeatedly until they can perform them automatically. This helps them to reduce to a minimum the number of errors that they make under stress in a game situation.

• Frequent changes of direction

The cones are positioned and the paths are specified to ensure that the players frequently have to change direction. In this way they learn to control their movements and the ball so well that they can move in any direction with the ball. They can only achieve this aim by carrying out lots of repetitions with lots of changes of direction.

At the same time they improve their ball control, which is the basis for numerous skills (control touch, passing technique, etc.).

The players should be able to control the ball so well that they can change direction at will while running with the ball or dribbling.

In game situations they should be able to make the right tactical decisions in response to the position of the nearest opponent. In other words they should be able to turn to the correct side and screen the ball while retaining close control.

• Frequently changing angle

As well as the frequent number of repetitions, the choice of various angles in a drill is also of key importance. By changing the circuit and the distances between the cones, a coach can ensure that his players are regularly confronted by new angles when they change direction.

Each new angle is a challenge:

For example, it is easier to change direction with the inside of the foot (p. 27) through an angle of 90 degrees than through 180 degrees (pp. 52, 53), as in the Comb.

At each angle, the best techniques for that specific angle can be practiced.

• Ability to use both feet

Players can be given tasks that encourage them to practice using both feet. If a player changes direction by playing the ball with the inside of his left foot at the first cone of the Zig-zag, for example, then he must change direction with the inside of his right foot at the next cone.

A player who is given the task of changing direction with the inside of his foot at each cone can only carry it out by using his right and left feet alternately.

During basic training sessions, in particular, it is important that the players use both feet, are capable of dribbling both right and left-footed, can feint to right and left, and can control the ball with the "weaker" foot.

When employing the Christmas Tree, Thunderbolt, Comb and Figure-8, it is essential to let the players start from both sides, so that they practice using both feet.

If, for example, a group starts the Comb on the right side and the players make a rotation with the inside of the foot at the right-angle, then they will have to use the left foot all the way round the circuit. The group should, therefore, start the next circuit on the left side. This ensures that the players practice mainly with the left foot during the first circuit and with the right during the second.

Another option would be to alternate between rotation (inside) and rotation (outside), as this also necessitates a change of foot.

• **Turns to right and left**

It sometimes happens that young players, in particular, become disoriented when they turn with the ball. They might then dribble to the wrong cone. For this reason, the rotation has a special place in the methodic sequence of basic movements.

It is advisable to let the players perform a rotation with the ball in their hands before trying it with the ball at their feet.

• **Meeting at the cones**

Before the players dribble for the first time in the P-S-S, the coach should tell them that they must always change direction before they reach a cone rather than dribbling past it first. They should also keep their distance from the cone, treating it like an opponent. If they do not do this, there is a danger that collisions will occur at the cones.

When the players change direction before they reach a cone, they are forced to raise their heads and make sure that they do not collide with players on the other side of the cone. Not only do the players take their eyes off the ball but they also have the feeling that they are training in a group, even though they are carrying out individual drills.

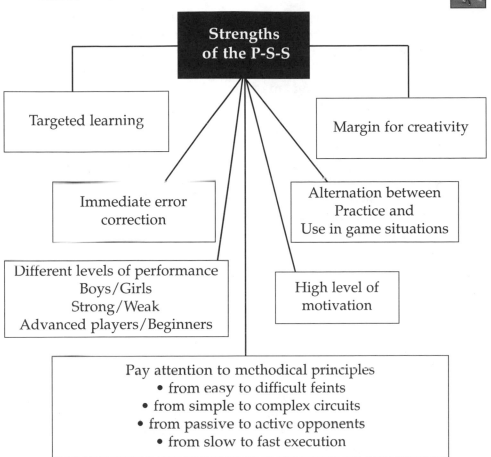

Strengths of the P-S-S

• Immediate error correction

All of the players participate within a single system. Each player has a ball and carries out the set tasks as well as he can. Beginners dribble the ball round the circuit slowly and deliberately, while more advanced players dribble at a faster pace.

The coach has all of the players in his field of view and can speak to each one directly. Errors can therefore be corrected selectively and immediately.

It is essential for coaches to take immediate corrective action, otherwise errors become firmly established and considerable effort is needed to eradicate them at a later stage. One advantage of the system is that the other players can continue with their drills when the coach intervenes to help an individual.

Errors that occur frequently should be discussed with the whole group. The best approach is for the coach to wait until the end of a lap, then point out the error and demonstrate how the movement should be carried out, or ask one of the players to demonstrate instead. The players can then practice during the following lap of the circuit.

• Targeted learning

The tasks and techniques are clearly formulated. The coach observes the players and can use the P-S-S to start a targeted learning process. Because all of the players in a learning phase use the same technique, the coach can immediately see whether the coaching objective has been achieved.

If the players need more practice to master a technique, the coach can give them additional drills as homework.

• Different levels of performance

Boys and girls (e.g. in schools), beginners and experts, stronger and weaker players - all of them can participate together in training sessions in the P-S-S, irrespective of the fact that they execute the drills at different speeds, have not all learned the same techniques, and sometimes use the techniques variably.

At the starting cone the coach can assign a more difficult task to a stronger player than to a weaker one. Another option is to ask the stronger player to carry out the drill as fast as possible. The distance between the two players would then have to be greater.

Another possible way of differentiating would be to set up a circuit with two starting points (e.g. a 4-fold Zig-zag, or a 4-fold Comb). A weaker group could start on the left with a simpler task, while the advanced group could start on the right with a more difficult task.

Different levels of workload can also be chosen. While the first group uses various techniques slowly, an advanced group can be asked to carry out basic movements so quickly that it finishes two rounds in the same time as the group of beginners.

• Methodical principles

The circuits and choice of feints depend on how advanced the players are. The tasks should force the players to carry out each drill with full concentration. The coach must ensure that his players are given an exact demonstration of the movements and that they can carry out the feints perfectly in slow motion before they become second nature through constant practice.

The level of difficulty of the feints, the complexity of the circuit, the speed of execution (pressure of time) and the involvement of an opponent (pressure of opposition) should be continuously increased.

• Room for creativity

Alongside the set tasks, effective coaching in dribbling skills should always leave room for players to express their own ideas and creatively apply the techniques they have learned. A coach should appreciate a player's spontaneous, spectacular trick just as much as a perfect feint that is part of the coaching plan. There should always be time to praise a player and to allow him to demonstrate his trick.

You will be surprised how inventive players can be.

• High level of motivation

Experience in clubs, schools and soccer schools has shown that players enjoy practicing basic movements. The P-S-S creates the basis for a high level of player motivation. This is reinforced when the players realize that their ball control is improving and that they have mastered attractive and spectacular techniques. They then practice the basic movements even more eagerly.

Changing the circuits and techniques ensures that training sessions never become boring. Under no circumstances, however, should the players be exposed to a surfeit of P-S-S. Like all things, practice is best in moderation.

• Alternation between practice and use in game situations

After their basic coaching, the players should be able to apply the feints they have learned in game situations. This can be done best in clearly defined game situations, then in games during training sessions, and then in real matches.

A player's coaching in dribbling skills can only be termed successful when he also uses these skills in real matches (see p. 24-25, Learning exercises).

What it takes to dribble successfully

Skills

Forward movement with the ball under close control

It is important for a player to be able to move forward unhurriedly with the ball always under control and close to his feet.

The player can focus on the situation around him, looking for the teammate who is in the best position to receive a pass or giving a teammate the opportunity to run into space. The player should be looking around rather than at the ball. The ball is propelled forward with the inside of the foot or the instep.

Running with the ball

Players must also be able to make a fast run while retaining control of the ball. The ball must not be as close to the feet as when moving forward more slowly but must always be under control. If necessary, the player must be able to change his speed or direction or even to stop suddenly.

Dribbling

Dribbling is the ability to retain control of the ball when under pressure from an opponent and to take the ball past an opponent. The ability to feint convincingly is an important aid to dribbling.

Feint

A feint is a movement that is intended to make an opponent move in the wrong direction. This is usually referred to as "sending an opponent the wrong way." A feint may involve any or all of the following: a change of pace; a change of direction; a body movement. A successful feint creates space for the player with the ball to dribble past an opponent.

Abilities

A good dribbler should
- be well coordinated and well balanced
- observe and anticipate the reactions of his opponent
- have good ball control skills
- have good awareness
- have mastered dribbling techniques and feints
- be able to time his feints correctly
- have good orientation

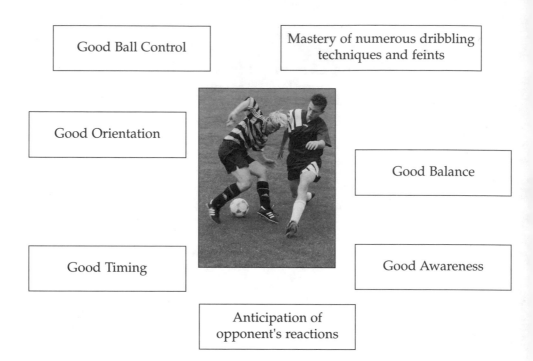

Good Ball Control	Mastery of numerous dribbling techniques and feints

Good Orientation

Good Balance

Good Timing

Good Awareness

Anticipation of opponent's reactions

Ten basic rules for good dribbling

1. An attacker who wants to dribble past a defender should first of all try to confuse his opponent with a feint. If the opponent reacts, the attacker immediately wins valuable time and space.
2. The dribbler's center of gravity should be as low to the ground as possible, allowing him to move in any direction from a stable starting position.
3. After the initial feint, the attacker's next move should be as dynamic as possible, to exploit the advantage that has been gained.
4. A skillful dribbler approaches an opponent from the side rather than from the front, and tries to tempt him to make a move for the ball. If the defender fails to make contact, he is off-balance and the attacker has gained the advantage. If the attacker feints to the right, for example, and the defender moves to block him, the defender has to stop and recover his balance before he can get back into position to stop the attacker. The split seconds won by the attacker may be sufficient to take the ball past the defender.
5. A skilled dribbler draws on his knowledge of his opponent and of his own particular strengths in selecting the feint he wants to use. A feint

is worthless if the defender does not react as expected. Moreover, there are feints that are especially suitable for fast attackers (e.g. on the wings, enabling the attacker to move into space) and others that are preferred by nimble players with especially good ball control (e.g. in the penalty area).

6. A dribbler should observe his opponent closely and be prepared to react immediately to any move he may make. If, for example, a defender fails to react to a feint and continues to block the direction in which the attacker originally intended to move, the attacker could instead move in the direction of the feint, or could make a second feint in an attempt to confuse the defender.

7. An attacker should not make a feint when he is too far away from his opponent. In other words, his opponent must not have time to recover after moving in the wrong direction. On the other hand, if a feint is made when the attacker is too close to the defender, the latter does not have enough time to react. As players gain experience in match situations, they acquire a feeling for the correct distance at which to make a feint. The dribbler should also take his opponent's speed of action and reaction into account.

8. A dribble should always be carried out for a purpose, in the interests of the team, and not for its own sake. A player who would rather "nutmeg" his opponent (take the ball past him by pushing it through his legs) than score a goal weakens his team, because he slows down its attacking moves. A dribble can, however, have a surprise effect that may decide a game. Players must learn not only how to dribble but also when.

9. Players should not dribble the ball when this could endanger their own goal. They should certainly avoid dribbling in their own penalty area! Dribbling always involves a risk of losing possession and should therefore be avoided if this could present the opposition with a chance of scoring a goal.

10. During a game, players should only use feints that they have frequently practiced and mastered. A poorly executed feint can destroy the dribbler's confidence.

When is dribbling a good option?

A dribble may be appropriate or even necessary
- if an attacker has no passing option
- to draw a defender out of position
- to create a shooting opportunity
- to waste time
- to make a breakthrough into free space
- to exploit a 1 against 1 situation close to the opposition's goal
- to open up space for an attack
- to give teammates time to push up
- to beat an offside trap

Learning to dribble

Creativity and Learning

The P-S-S system is a coaching method that provides a coach with a systematic learning program and corresponding organizational forms (circuits) and descriptions. The coach can use it to plan his players' learning process economically and logically.

The following information is of importance for learning sports movements.

Creativity requires a large repertoire of movements

Basic movements are taught and practiced purposefully, effectively and methodically until they become automatic. The players practice important movements, which are always carried out in the same sequence, so intensively and variedly that they can perform them reliably, almost automatically, in a variety of game situations.

A broad repertoire of movements gives a player a range of options from which to choose and is a basis for creative play. Only when a player has mastered a variety of feints to both right and left, together with the appropriate follow-up moves, can he take the ball past his opponent in a 1 to 1 situation or even put a whole defense on the wrong foot.

This does not mean that a player should not focus on a particular trick that he can perform especially well. He should, however, know how to hide his intentions from his opponent until the very last moment.

Learning sports movements

Young soccer players should not learn soccer movements randomly, as is so often still the case. Many coaches work without a long-term coaching plan, and simply decide on the content of their coaching sessions from week to week or session to session. The content of their coaching sessions is often random. Many coaches feel that they do not have the qualifications needed to devise a child-oriented, systematic and methodical coaching plan.

P-S-S provides these coaches with a plan for teaching young players feinting, dribbling and ball control skills.

Players must be shown exactly how to carry out a movement before they make their own first approximate attempts. First of all they should be shown the sequence of the movement, then the movements of the individual parts of the body must be explained.

The movement can be demonstrated, or the players can be shown a video or the illustrations in this book, etc.

Sketches, photos, photo series

A coach could, for example, take this book with him to the sports facility, show his players the relevant illustrations, and give them copies to take home and study.

Naturally, such homework can only be assigned if the players are able and willing to work on their own. They could practice movements or be given a problem to solve. For example, they could be asked to devise a combination of various feints.

Moving images (videos, films)

The movements can be shown smoothly in their entirety.

In addition, the coach can make use of stills, slow motion and any number of repeats. Because a lot of equipment is needed (videotape recorder and television, or film projector and screen), the demonstration will often have to be given at a venue other than the sports facility. There will therefore be a gap between seeing and practicing. The coach should carefully consider the amount of information that his players can absorb and the type of language that they can best understand. This will depend on their age and the current level of their soccer "education."

Visual material should be discussed briefly, without going into too much detail. It is often advisable to focus only on the most important points at first and leave a discussion of the details until later.

The terminology of the P-S-S is clear and easily understandable, even for 8-year-olds.

Demonstrations

• **Technically perfect**

A demonstration should be technically perfect. It is therefore better to ask a player with a good technique to demonstrate it than for a coach to demonstrate it imperfectly himself.

It is often sufficient to simply indicate how a new movement should be carried out. Talented players will quickly grasp what is required and can then demonstrate this to their teammates.

• **Repeating difficult movements**

Particularly difficult movements should be repeated several times. The coach can ask the players to carry out various tasks so that he can see whether they have really understood the separate parts of the movement.

• **Focus on individual parts of the body or slow motion**

Sometimes it is advisable to focus on one part of the body. Important phases of a movement can be carried out slowly to help the players to identify and understand what is required of them.

• **Field of vision**

The coach should ensure that the players have a good field of vision, so that they can observe the movement properly. The distance and angle of vision are important.

Correcting errors

The coach should correct the errors that he observes during the coaching sessions, paying special attention to the following points:

His comments should be brief and to the point.

- Errors should be dealt with one after the other, not simultaneously.
- Emphasize the important aspects. Avoid too much detail, as this could confuse and demotivate the players.
- Encourage the players with calls such as "Well done!" and "That's right!"
- Errors can be dealt with after a practice run, when all of the players have carried out a drill and are in a receptive mood. If, however, it is immediately obvious that the players have misunderstood what is wanted, the coach should halt the drill immediately and explain it more clearly before restarting.
- Individual errors can also be corrected during a drill. The correction should take the form of short, clear instructions.

Ways of correcting errors

- Let the players compare two movements (one wrong, one correct) and identify the error themselves. The coach can draw their attention to errors by asking suitable questions.
- The coach can ask the players to carry out additional drills designed to eradicate errors. For example, players who keep their eyes too firmly directed at the ball at their feet could be asked to watch for signals from the coach while they carry out a movement.
- A demonstration can be repeated, drawing the players' attention to the critical elements.
- If the players fail to carry out a complex drill correctly, the appropriate preliminary drills or parts of the whole sequence should be repeated.

Learning exercises

The following sequence has proved effective for learning feints.
1. The player should be given a clear picture of the movement with the help of photos, videos or demonstrations by fellow players or the coach.
2. A new movement should be practiced slowly by the player on his own.

When he can perform it correctly, he must learn to carry it out automatically by practicing it in a variety of circuits. Players feint automatically when a game situation requires this, or build up to a feint consciously if they have sufficient time. In either case the player must be able to carry out the movement automatically before he can use it in a game situation while retaining his overview of the game situation. Players must also learn to observe and react to an opponent automatically by carrying out any of a variety of feints.

3. A passive or partially active defender should be introduced into practice drills to make them more "real" and allow attackers to learn how to position themselves at the correct distance from a defender and how to time a feint correctly. These aspects require a lot of practice and experience.

4. When players have mastered a feint, it must be practiced in small sided games, in realistic game situations and, of course, in real games.

5. From the very start, it is advisable to practice feints in typical game situations and demonstrate possible ways of using them. The players should understand the purpose of a feint.

6. The ultimate aim is to use techniques in real games once they have been mastered. A player can only demonstrate that he has really mastered a trick by carrying it out under pressure from an opponent under competitive conditions.

Basic movements

Youngsters should learn the key basic movements at an early age so that they will subsequently be able to master complex sequences of movements. Time and patience are required to acquire good ball control, a repertoire of feints and the ability to use them in game situations.

Attacker facing defender

An attacker faced by an opponent has no teammates available to receive a pass, or realizes that his most promising option is to dribble for goal or down the flank or into space in midfield.

First of all he has to take the ball past his opponent. Soccer players frequently find themselves in this sort of stress situation during a game. Usually they do not possess the technical skills to exploit it.

As a result, they are forced to pass the ball to a colleague who is probably equally incapable of dribbling past an opponent.

Spectacular dribbles and surprising individual runs that put a complete defense on the wrong foot have become rarities on our soccer pitches.

The best age to start learning the following basic movements is between 9 and 12 years. They should subsequently be practiced regularly and perfected, so that they become second nature.

Change of direction (inside of foot)

A player can use the inside of the foot to change the direction of the ball through any angle up to 180 degrees. The variations range from a slight change of direction to enable the attacker to take the ball past an opponent, to a reverse of a previous change of direction to enable the attacker to continue his run in the original direction. An effective variant is a fast change of direction preceded by a feint to shoot. This can draw an opponent into a sliding tackle and leave him skidding helplessly past the ball. A double or even a triple change of direction is very simple and effective and can leave a defender dizzy.

A change of direction is often preceded by a feint to shoot, which can win the attacker a few extra seconds.

(a) The player runs towards the cone with the ball at his feet.

(b) He positions his right foot behind the ball.

(c) He plays the ball to his left with the inside of his right foot, then sprints to the next cone with the ball at his feet.

Change of direction (outside of foot)

Changing direction with the outside of the foot is more difficult than with the inside of the foot. Beginners find that the ball sometimes rolls over the foot. The movement often looks stiff, wooden and inelegant.

Changing direction with the outside of the foot makes more demands on the ankles and hips and requires some initial familiarization.

Typical errors

When youngsters first practice changing direction with the outside of the foot, they sometimes continue to play the ball with the side of the foot as they run from cone to cone.

Correction instruction

Push the ball forward using both feet as usual when running from one cone to the next.

(a) The player runs towards the cone with the ball at his feet.

(b) He positions his right foot to the right of the ball.

(c) He draws his left foot into position between his right foot and the ball, then plays the ball to the left with the outside of his left foot.

(d) He sprints away with the ball.

Dummy step

The feint (in this case, the dummy step to the right) is intended to make the opponent think that the attacker intends to pass or make a run to the right. However, the player does not play the ball but continues the fast movement of his right foot from right-to-left across and behind the ball. With his weight on his right foot, the player then pushes the ball suddenly to his left and sprints away with the ball at his feet, leaving his opponent behind him.

Typical errors

The player does not carry out the dummy step or the run with the ball convincingly enough. When the players have mastered this key basic movement at the cone to the stage where they can carry it out automatically, they often forget that the cone is supposed to represent an opponent.

Correction instruction

The coach must always ensure that the players carry out the necessary movements dynamically and remind them to carry them out convincingly.

"Carry out the dummy step and run with the ball dynamically and convincingly! Sprint away from the cone!"

Dummy step (outside-outside)

(a) The player runs towards the cone and feints to shoot or make a run.

(b) He puts his right foot to the ground, to the right of the ball, and transfers his weight to this foot.

(c) He draws his left foot into position between his right leg and the ball, then plays the ball to the left with the outside of his left foot.

(d) He sprints away from his opponent.

Dummy step (outside-inside)

The dummy step to the right can be followed up by pushing the ball to the left with the inside of the right foot. It is then called a dummy step (outside-inside) and is carried out by feinting to play the ball with the outside of the right foot, then actually playing it with the inside of the right foot. No change of foot occurs, because the ball is played with the foot that makes the dummy step.

(a) The player runs towards the cone with the ball at his feet, then makes a dummy step to the right, placing his right foot to the right of the ball.

(b) He leans to the left, transferring his weight to his left foot.

(c) He plays the ball to his left with the inside of his right foot.

Dummy step (inside-outside)

The dummy step from left to right, leading with the left leg, is frequently used when an attacker takes the ball slowly towards an opponent or stands facing an opponent.

The attacker takes a dummy step with his left foot. In other words, he feints to make a run or pass the ball with the inside of his left foot.

After transferring his weight to his right leg, however, he takes the ball back to his left with the outside of his left foot and sprints away from his opponent in the new direction.

(a) The player runs towards the cone with the ball at his feet, then feints to make a run or pass the ball with the inside of his left foot.

(b) He puts his left foot to the ground, to the right of the ball, then takes a step forward with his right foot.

(c) He transfers his weight to his right leg, then plays the ball to his left with the outside of his left foot.

Dummy step (inside-inside)

In contrast to the dummy step (inside-outside), in this case the movement is continued by playing the ball with the inside of the foot. This variant may be necessary as a response to the defender's reaction. The attacker should always watch his opponent closely and pay attention to each movement of his feet, especially in the direction of the ball. He must respond quickly to keep the ball out of reach of the defender's challenge.

(a) The player runs towards the cone with the ball at his feet, then feints to make a run or pass the ball with the inside of the left foot.

(b) He continues the left to right movement of his left foot behind the ball, placing his left foot to the right of the ball.

(c) He transfers his weight to his left leg, then swivels to the left, swinging his right foot towards the ball.

(d) He pushes the ball to the left with the inside of his right foot and sprints away from his opponent.

Step-over

Step-over (outside-outside)

If a player feints by stepping over the ball rather than behind it, this is called a step-over. The movements are similar to those of the dummy step, and the two are frequently confused. Of the four possible feints, only the step-overs aimed at making a defender expect the attacker to make a run or pass the ball with the outside of the foot are described here.

After the step-over, the ball is played with either the outside (outside-outside) or the inside (outside-inside) of the foot.

(a) The player runs towards the cone with the ball at his feet.

(b) He feints to make a run or pass the ball with the outside of the right foot.

(c) He steps over the ball, placing his right foot to the right of it, and transfers his weight to the right foot.

(d) He draws his left leg towards his right leg, positioning it between his right leg and the ball, then plays the ball to his left with the outside of his left foot.

Step-over (outside-inside)

The step-over can also be continued with the inside of the step-over foot. The movement is then a step-over (outside-inside). The player must step over the ball dynamically and convincingly with his right foot, transfer his weight to his left leg and play the ball suddenly to his left with the inside of his right foot.

(a) The player runs towards the cone with the ball at his feet and feints to make a run or pass the ball with the outside of the right foot.

(b) He steps over the ball with his right foot and puts it to the ground, to the right of the ball.

(c) He braces his right leg to brake his momentum to the right, then transfers his weight to his left leg.

(d) He plays the ball to his left with the inside of his right foot and sprints away from his opponent.

Step-over (inside-outside) (no illustrations)

A player carrying out a step-over (inside-outside) feints to play the ball with the inside of one foot, then plays it in the opposite direction with the outside of the same foot.

Step-over (inside-inside) (no illustrations)

A player carrying out a step-over (inside-inside) feints to play the ball with the inside of one foot, then plays it in the opposite direction with the inside of the other foot.

Scissor

Scissor (inside-outside) (Rivelino trick)

A player carrying out a scissor (inside-outside) swings one foot across the front of the ball, feinting to make a run or pass the ball with the inside of this foot. He then continues the movement with the outside of the same foot. This movement is termed a scissor (inside-outside).

The Brazilian, Rivelino, used this feint frequently, so it can also be called the Rivelino trick.

The scissor (outside-outside) and the scissor (outside-inside) are not shown here, but can be easily derived from the step-over (pp. 34/35).

(a) The player feints to make a run or pass the ball with the inside of the left foot, but takes the foot across the front of the ball.

(b) He puts his left foot to the ground, to the right of the ball.

(c) He takes one step with his right foot and turns to the left.

(d) He transfers his weight to his right leg and plays the ball to his left with the outside of his left foot.

Scissor (inside-inside)

If, after the feint with the inside of the left foot, the player continues the movement with the inside of the right foot, the movement is referred as a scissor (inside-inside).

The player quickly transfers his weight to his left foot, turns to the left and sprints away from his opponent.

(a) The player feints to make a run or pass the ball with the inside of the left foot, but takes the foot across the front of the ball.

(b) He puts his left foot to the ground.

(c) He swivels to the left on his left leg.

(d) He plays the ball to the left with the inside of his right foot.

Scissor (outside-outside) (no illustrations)

The player takes the outside of one foot around the front of the ball and puts it to the ground. He then plays the ball in the opposite direction with the outside of the other foot (see Step-over (outside-outside) on p. 34).

Scissor (outside-inside) (no illustrations)

The initial feint is the same as for the scissor (outside-outside), but the movement is continued with the inside of the same foot (see Step-over (outside-inside) on p. 35).

The foot on the ball trick

The foot on the ball trick is often preceded by a feint to shoot. The player shapes up to shoot, then suddenly places his foot on the ball, drags the ball back, away from his opponent, and plays the ball in another direction, either with the instep or the inside of the foot.

Foot on the ball trick (instep)

(a) The player stops the ball by placing the sole of his left foot on it.

(b) He drags the ball back with the sole of his left foot.

(c) He draws his left foot towards his right leg until it is positioned between the right leg and the ball, then plays the ball to his left with his left instep.

(d) He sprints away from the cone with the ball at his feet.

Foot on the ball trick
(inside of the foot, away from the standing leg)

There are two ways of carrying out the foot on the ball trick with the inside of the foot. If the attacker wants to keep as much distance between himself and his opponent as possible, he should turn away from his standing leg. In other words, he should turn left if he is standing on his right leg, and vice versa. As he turns, he can drag the ball a considerable distance back, because the space behind the ball is free.

(a) The player runs towards the cone with the ball at his feet and feints to shoot.

(b) He stops the ball by placing the sole of his left foot on it.

(c) He drags the ball back with the sole of his left foot.

(d) He turns to the left and plays the ball to the left with the inside of his left foot. He sprints away from the cone with the ball at his feet.

Foot on the ball trick
(inside of the foot, across the standing leg)

When a player carries out the foot on the ball trick and takes the ball across the front of the standing leg, he has to move very nimbly. This is because the standing leg is initially in the path of the ball. The player thus has to move his standing leg out of the way of the ball to carry out the movement successfully.

(a) The player feints to shoot.

(b) He stops the ball by placing the sole of his right foot on it.

(c) He drags the ball back with the sole of his right foot.

(d) He plays the ball to the left with the inside of his right foot.

(e) He moves the standing leg (in this case the left leg) back out of the path of the ball.

(f) He sprints away from the cone with the ball at his feet.

40

Foot on the ball trick
(behind the standing leg)

In this variant of the foot on the ball trick, the ball is dragged back behind the standing leg and then played at right angles behind the standing leg. The standing leg thus screens the ball from the opponent.

(a) The player runs towards the cone with the ball at his feet and feints to shoot.

(b) He stops the ball by placing the sole of his right foot on it, then drags the ball back with the sole of his right foot.

(c) In one fluid movement, he drags the ball behind the standing leg.

(d) He turns to his left and sprints away from the cone with the ball at his feet.

Rotation (inside)

Rotation is simply a repeated change of direction, with the first change of direction taking place in the opposite direction to the one that the player ultimately intends to take. If the player wants to take the ball to the left, he changes direction to the right, with his body screening the ball from his opponent. He continues changing direction to the right until he can sprint away to the left of his initial direction. A rotation can be very effectively preceded by a feint to shoot.

Rotation (inside) without initial feint

(a) The player runs towards the cone with the ball at his feet, then swings his left foot forward until it is at the left side of the ball.

(b) He uses the inside of the left foot to play the ball to the right and simultaneously turns to the right.

(c) He makes a second and third change of direction to the right.

(d) He continues the rotation around the right leg.

(e) He sprints away to the left of the cone with the ball at his feet.

Scissor (inside) and rotation (inside)

Players with good ball control can precede the scissor with a feint. The following photo sequence shows a scissor (inside) preceded by a rotation (inside).

(a) The player runs towards the cone with the ball at his feet, then carries out a scissor (inside) with the right foot.

(b) He puts his right foot to the ground, then swivels clockwise on his right foot, thus bringing the inside of his left foot behind the ball.

(c) He plays the ball across his standing leg with the inside of his right foot.

(d) He continues the rotation, plays the ball in the new direction with the inside of his left foot and sprints away from the cone with the ball at his feet.

Dummy step (outside) and rotation (inside)

The rotation (inside) can be preceded by a dummy step (outside).

(a) The player runs towards the cone with the ball at his feet, then takes a dummy step with the left foot.

(b) He puts his left foot to the ground and transfers his weight to it.

(c) He leans back to the right, transferring his weight to his right foot, then plays the ball around his standing leg with the inside of his left foot.

(d) He continues the rotation, then plays the ball in the new direction with the inside of his left foot and sprints away from the cone with the ball at his feet.

Rotation (outside)

The rotation (outside) is more difficult than the rotation (inside). The outside of the foot must be twisted across the front of the ball to start the rotation. Franz Beckenbauer made frequent use of this movement.

Rotation (outside) without initial feint

(a) The player runs towards the cone with the ball at his feet, then twists the outside of his right foot around the front of the ball and plays the ball to his right.

(b) He takes a pace forward with his left foot, to which he transfers his weight.

(c) He swivels to the right, always changing the direction of the ball by playing it with the outside of his right foot.

(d) He sprints away from the cone with the ball at his feet.

Scissor (inside) and rotation (outside)

Advanced players can precede the rotation (outside) with a scissor (inside)

(a) The player runs towards the cone with the ball at his feet, then carries out a scissor with the inside of the right foot.

(b) He puts his right foot to the ground and starts to swivel to the right, swinging his left foot around his right leg.

(c) He puts his left leg to the ground and plays the ball to the right with the outside of his right foot. He continues the rotation with a series of changes of direction to the right, finally playing the ball in the new direction of his run (i.e., to the left of his original direction).

(d) He sprints away from the cone with the ball at his feet.

Dummy step (outside) and rotation (outside)

Some players prefer to initiate the rotation (outside) with a dummy step (outside). A complete player, however, will have mastered both movements.

(a) The player starts by carrying out a dummy step with the left foot.

(b) He puts the left foot to the ground, takes one pace to brace himself and draws his right foot towards his left leg, positioning it between the ball and his left leg.

(c) He carries out a change of direction to the right by playing the ball with the outside of his right foot.

(d) He continues the rotation with a series of changes of direction to the right, always using the outside of his right foot to play the ball.

(e) He plays the ball in the new direction of his run and sprints away from the cone with the ball at his feet.

Matthews trick

The legendary English international player, Stanley Matthews, had a special trick with which he outsmarted many a defender. As an outside-right, he would feint to dart inside by taking a pace to his left, playing the ball in the same direction with the inside of his right foot. If the opponent responded to this feint by taking a step to the right to follow the ball, Matthews would suddenly use the outside of his right foot to tap the ball in the opposite direction and then take it past the off-balance defender on the outside. He would then sprint down the right flank and cross the ball.

(a) The attacker feints to make a run inside by tapping the ball to the left with the inside of the right foot.

(b) He transfers his weight to his left leg and immediately taps the ball to his right with the outside of his right foot.

(c) He uses the outside of the right foot to either flick the ball over the defender's outstretched left leg or push the ball past him along the ground.

(d) He sprints after the ball, leaving the defender behind.

Attacker to side of defender
(180-degree change of direction)

The Comb (see pp. 116-118), in particular, is suitable for practicing a 180-degree change of direction until it becomes automatic.

Players should master these basic movements so that they will be able to shake off, or take the ball past, an opponent who challenges from the side.

In addition, the players improve their touch and ball control skills in difficult game situations. When the players have mastered the basic movements for 180-degree changes of direction, the coach should let them practice these movements in suitable game situations (e.g. a blocked run down the flank or a challenge from the side). In this way the players can learn to associate the drill with a real game and will be able to use the techniques against a defender.

The coach should also include alternative follow-up movements in his coaching program. An attacker who feints successfully, for example, can follow this up by passing to a teammate or by continuing his run and shooting at goal.

Practicing with both feet

All drills should be practiced with both the right and left foot.

It is important for an attacker to use the foot that is furthest away from the defender to drag the ball back. Thus, if a defender challenges from the attacker's left side, the attacker should drag the ball back with his right foot.

In the illustrations the players turn in only one direction. Players should, however, practice and master turning in both directions, because a challenge can come from either the right or the left. The attacker's choice of foot for dragging the ball back, and the direction in which he turns, depend on the direction from which the challenge comes.

If a defender challenges from the attacker's right, for example, then the player should drag the ball back with his left foot, drop his left shoulder and turn to the left, so that his body immediately screens the ball again (see photos on pp. 50/51).

Drag-back with the sole of the foot

A player runs with the ball at his feet towards a mark, places his foot briefly on the ball and suddenly drags the ball back with the sole of his foot. At the same time he turns through 180 degrees. He then runs with the ball at his feet to the cone from which he started.

This technique could be important for a winger who wants to cross the ball, but whose path forward is blocked by a defender.

The winger feints to cross, but instead puts his foot on the ball and drags it back, turns round and moves back towards his own goal. He now has the option of passing the ball inside, crossing the ball, or, if drag-back leaves the challenging defender lying on the ground, dribbling round the defender and shooting at goal.

This method of carrying out a 180-degree turn with the ball is especially suitable for beginners, because the ball is relatively easy to control. The coach should repeatedly encourage his players to increase the speed with which they carry out the drag-back and turn.

Drag-back with the sole of the foot and counterclockwise turn

(a) The player runs towards the cone with the ball at his feet and feints to shoot (in this case with the right foot).

(b) He stops the ball by placing his right foot on it, then drags the ball back with the sole of his right foot.

(c) With his weight on his left foot, he quickly turns counterclockwise through 180 degrees.

(d) He sprints to the next cone with the ball at his feet.

Drag-back with the sole of the foot and clockwise turn

(a) The player runs towards the cone with the ball at his feet and feints to shoot (in this case with his left foot).

(b) He stops the ball by placing his left foot on it, then drags the ball back with the sole of his left foot.

(c) With his weight on his right foot, he quickly turns clockwise through 180 degrees.

(d) He sprints to the next cone with the ball at his feet.

Change of direction (inside)

The change of direction with the inside of the foot is, together with the drag-back with the sole, the simplest method of changing the direction of the ball by 180 degrees.

The player runs towards the cone with the ball at his feet, swings the inside of his foot round the ball, and sprints back to the previous cone with the ball at his feet.

Change of direction (inside) with clockwise turn

(a) The player runs towards the cone with the ball at his feet.

(b) He swings his left foot round the left side of the ball and plays the ball in the reverse direction with the inside of this foot.

(c) He stops his forward movement and turns clockwise through 180 degrees.

(d) He sprints to the next cone with the ball at his feet.

Change of direction (inside) with counterclockwise turn

(a) The player runs towards the cone with the ball at his feet.

(b) He swings his right foot round the right side of the ball and plays the ball to his left with the inside of this foot.

(c) He stops his forward movement and turns counterclockwise through 180 degrees.

(d) He sprints to the next cone with the ball at his feet.

Change of direction (outside)

A forward-backward movement (180-degree change of direction) can also be carried out with the outside of the foot. This technique is more difficult and requires supple hips, knees and ankles.

This is called a change of direction (outside).

Change of direction (outside) with clockwise turn

(a) The player runs towards the cone with the ball at his feet and feints to shoot.

(b) He swings his right foot round the left side of the ball and drags the ball to his right with the outside of this foot.

(c) He stops his forward movement and turns clockwise through 180 degrees.

(d) He sprints to the next cone with the ball at his feet.

Change of direction (outside) with counterclockwise turn

(a) The player runs towards the cone with the ball at his feet and feints to shoot. He swings his left foot round the right side of the ball and drags the ball to his left.

(b) He stops his forward movement and turns counterclockwise through 180 degrees.

(c) He sprints to the next cone with the ball at his feet.

Scissor

The scissor is a feint in which the foot passes across the front of the ball. The player feints to pass the ball with the inside of his foot, but continues the foot movement across the front of the ball without touching the ball. He transfers his weight to this foot, then swivels suddenly and plays the ball in the reverse direction with the inside of the other foot. This feint can be used when a defender runs towards the ball with an opponent to one side of him. He feints to pass the ball back to his goalkeeper or another teammate, but carries out a scissor and suddenly sprints away with the ball in the reverse direction. He must be sure to run away from, and not towards, his opponent.

Scissor (inside-inside)

(a) The player runs towards the cone with the ball at his feet, and feints to shoot with the inside of his right foot, but swings this foot across the front of the ball without touching it.

(b) He puts his right foot to the ground, then swivels to his right, swinging his left leg around behind the ball.

(c) He plays the ball in the new direction with the inside of his left foot.

(d) He turns in the new direction, keeping the ball under close control.

(e) He sprints to the next cone with the ball at his feet.

Scissor (inside-outside)

This basic technique requires no change of foot. The scissor movement around the front of the ball and the continuation of the movement are carried out with the same foot.

(a) The player runs towards the cone with the ball at his feet.

(b) He feints to shoot with the inside of his right foot, but swings his right foot from right to left across the front of the ball without touching the ball.

(c) He transfers his weight to his left foot, then draws his right foot back towards the ball.

(d) He plays the ball in the reverse direction with the outside of his right foot.

(e) He turns in the new direction, keeping the ball under close control, and sprints to the next cone with the ball at his feet.

Scissor (outside-outside)

(a) The player runs towards the cone with the ball at his feet. He feints to shoot with the outside of his left foot, but swings his left foot from right to left across the front of the ball.

(b) He puts his left foot to the ground and transfers his weight to this foot.

(c) He swings his right foot round the left side of the ball.

(d) He plays the ball in the reverse direction with the outside of his right foot and turns to the right.

(e) He plays the ball in the new direction and sprints to the next cone with the ball at his feet.

Scissor (outside-inside)

As with the scissor (inside-outside), the scissor movement around the front of the ball and the continuation of the movement are carried out with the same foot.

(a) The player runs with the ball towards the cone.

(b) He feints to shoot with the outside of his left foot, but swings this foot across the front of the ball from right to left.

(c) He takes a pace with his left foot, then with his right foot, and transfers his weight to the right foot. He then swivels to his right, swinging his left foot behind the ball.

(d) He plays the ball in the reverse direction with the inside of his left foot.

(e) He turns in the new direction and sprints to the next cone with the ball at his feet.

Dragging the ball behind the standing leg

The most interesting technique for turning through 180 degrees is shown in the photo sequence below. The player drags the ball behind his standing leg, turns suddenly and runs with the ball in the opposite direction. Johan Cruyff used this technique perfectly. He frequently preceded it by feinting to shoot.

When Cruyff's opponent took a step in the desired direction, Cruyff turned his foot inward and dragged the ball back with the front of the foot. After a rapid turn he would sprint into space with the ball, leaving his opponent stranded. The standing leg screens the ball during this movement.

(a) The player runs with the ball towards the cone and feints to shoot.

(b) With both knees slightly bent, he turns his left foot inward across the front of the ball.

(c) With the front of his left foot he flicks the ball backward.

(d) He puts his left foot to the ground, turns clockwise and plays the ball with his right foot.

60

Drag behind the standing leg - counterclockwise turn

(a) The player runs towards the cone with the ball at his feet and feints to shoot.

(b) With both knees slightly bent, he turns the right foot inward across the front of the ball.

(c) With the front of the right foot he flicks the ball backward.

(d) He puts his right foot to the ground, turns counterclockwise and plays the ball with his left foot.

"Leo" trick

The Leo trick involves feinting to back-heel the ball, slowing down, and then suddenly sprinting forward with the ball under close control. The player takes the back-heel foot back over the ball, then suddenly uses his instep to play the ball forward. The change of pace causes the opponent to slow down and the attacker uses this moment to accelerate again and leave his opponent behind. Wingers often use this trick when they are close to the sideline (see photo sequence on p. 84).

Attacker with back to defender

An attacker expects a pass from a teammate. He stands with his back to goal and is closely marked by a defender. This is not an easy situation. The attacker cannot see how his marker reacts and is under intense pressure. This can make young players, in particular, very nervous, and as a result they may make mistakes and lose possession.

When the pass is made, the attacker can react to it in four ways.

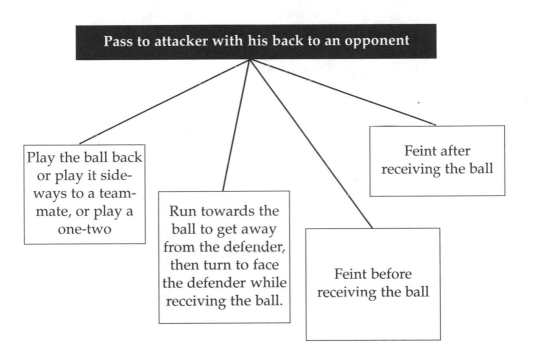

Pass to attacker with his back to an opponent

Play the ball back or play it sideways to a teammate, or play a one-two

Run towards the ball to get away from the defender, then turn to face the defender while receiving the ball.

Feint after receiving the ball

Feint before receiving the ball

1. The attacker could immediately play the ball back or to the side, then get away from his marker (perhaps by feinting to run in one direction then running in another) and ask for the ball again. This could result in a one-two. If the attacker screens the ball while he lays it off, this makes it very difficult for the defender to challenge and win the ball.
2. The attacker could run to meet the ball, thus putting space between himself and his opponent, so that he can turn to face his opponent as he receives the ball. He can then try to dribble past his opponent. An attacker can gain space by feinting to run in another direction before he runs to meet the ball (see photos on p. 63).

Receiving the ball and turning

(a) The attacker feints to run to the right to put the defender off-balance, then runs to meet the ball.

(b) The attacker starts to turn to his left as he receives the ball on his left foot.

(c) He continues his turn to the left as he controls the ball with his left foot.

(d) He drags the ball to the left with the inside of his left foot as he finishes his turn to face his opponent.

(e) He dribbles past his opponent, who is now facing him.

3. A feint (e.g. a dummy step) can be a very effective way of gaining space before receiving the ball (see photo sequence below and on the next page). The defender is drawn to the wrong side and the attacker takes the ball smoothly in the opposite direction. The attacker should try not to allow the ball to bounce off his foot. This is especially likely to happen if the ball is moving at speed. The attacker should try to screen the ball as well as possible and keep it under close control. The aim is to use the body to prevent the opponent from challenging for the ball.

(a) The attacker takes a dummy step to the left to draw his opponent off balance.

(b) He screens the ball.

(c) He takes the ball on the run and screens it from his opponent.

(d) He sprints away from his opponent and shoots at goal or passes to a teammate.

First touch with the outside of the foot

The attacker screens the approaching ball with his body, then takes the ball on the run with the outside of his right foot.

(a) The situation just before the attacker takes the ball with the outside of his right foot.

(b) The attacker sprints towards the goal or down the wing.

First touch with the outside of the foot (view from the side)

(a) The attacker watches the ball closely and adjusts his position to its path. He takes the ball with the outside of his right foot while turning to the right.

(b) He stops the turn and keeps the ball under close control.

(c) He sprints in the new direction.

4. An attacker is frequently challenged from behind by an opponent just as he receives the ball. In this situation he should screen the ball, take one or two dummy steps and dribble past his opponent (see photos below). A dribble can be preceded by moving slowly with the ball to tempt the opponent into making a challenge. This will increase the chance of success of a sudden change of direction.

(a) The attacker controls the ball while screening it from the defender.

(b) He feints [this photo shows a scissor (inside-inside)].

(c) He dribbles past the defender and sprints into space.

To be successful in situations where a feint is called for after receiving the ball, a player should learn certain basic movements that will enable him to dribble with the ball under control when under pressure, and to take his eyes off the ball to observe the defender's responses even when he has his back to the defender.

Dummy step

Dummy step (outside-outside)

(a) The attacker makes a dummy step to the left with his left foot. The defender responds by making a step in the same direction.

(b) The attacker transfers his weight to the left foot and swings his right foot between the ball and his left foot.

(c) He plays the ball to the right with the outside of his right foot and turns in the new direction.

(d) He sprints away from the defender.

Dummy step (outside-inside)

(a) The attacker takes a dummy step to his left with his left foot.

(b) He puts his left foot to the ground, then plays the ball to his right with the inside of his left foot.

(c) He keeps his body between the ball and the defender.

(d) He sprints away from the defender.

Dummy step (inside-outside)

(a) The attacker's body screens the ball from the defender.

(b) The attacker takes a dummy step to his left with his right foot. The defender responds by taking a step in the same direction.

(c) The attacker braces himself with his left foot and then plays the ball in the reverse direction with the outside of his right foot.

(d) He sprints away from the defender.

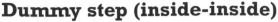

Dummy step (inside-inside)

(a) The attacker's body screens the ball from the defender. With his right foot, the attacker feints to pass or make a run to his left.

(b) The attacker takes a dummy step to his left with his right foot. The defender responds by taking a step in the same direction.

(c) The attacker braces himself with his left foot and then plays the ball to his right with the inside of his left foot.

(d) He sprints away from the defender.

Step-over
Step-over (outside-outside)

(a) The attacker steps over the ball with his left foot.

(b) He puts his left foot to the ground, while screening the ball from the defender.

(c) He then suddenly moves to the right and plays the ball to the right with the outside of his right foot.

(d) He sprints away from the defender.

Step-over (outside-inside), taking the ball with the inside of the foot

(a) The attacker turns to the right, swinging his left foot across his standing leg to play the ball with the inside of his left foot.

(b) Still screening the ball, he plays it in the new direction and sprints away from the defender.

71

Step-over (inside-outside)

(a) The attacker steps over the ball with his right foot.

(b) He then braces himself with his left foot, screening the ball from the defender.

(c) He then turns to the right and plays the ball to his right with the outside of his right foot.

(d) Still screening the ball, he plays it in the new direction and sprints away from the defender.

Step-over (inside-inside)

(a) The attacker steps over the ball from right to left with his right foot.

(b) He puts his right foot to the ground, then takes a further step with his left foot, so that the left foot is further away from the ball than the right.

(c) He then leans to the right, transferring his weight to his right foot.

(d) He swivels to the right with his weight on his right foot, plays the ball in the new direction with the inside of his left foot, and sprints away from the defender.

Scissor (outside-outside)

(a) The attacker screens the ball from the defender.

(b) The attacker swings his left foot from right to left across the front of the ball.

(c) He puts his left foot to the ground, transfers his weight to it and immediately plays the ball to his right with the outside of his right foot. He then makes a run away from the defender.

Scissor (outside-inside)

(a) The attacker screens the ball from the defender.

(b) The attacker swings his left foot from right to left across the front of the ball, feinting to make a run to the left.

(c) He puts his left foot to the ground, leans to the right, transfers his weight to his right foot and immediately plays the ball to his right with the inside of his left foot.

(d) He then sprints away from the defender.

Scissor (inside-outside)

(a) The attacker swings his right foot from right to left across the front of the ball.

(b) He puts his right foot to the ground, then transfers his weight to his left foot.

(c) He turns to the right and plays the ball to his right with the outside of his right foot.

(d) He then sprints away from the defender.

Scissor (inside-inside)

(a) The attacker feints to make a run or shoot with his right foot.

(b) He swings his right foot from right to left across the front of the ball.

(c) He puts his right foot to the ground and then swivels to the right, swinging his left leg round and behind the ball.

(d) He plays the ball with the inside of his left foot and sprints away from the defender.

Putting basic movements into practice

Players should be given as many opportunities as possible to use their newly acquired techniques in small sided games (5 v 5) and in game situations set up by the coach. The creative use of difficult techniques in game situations involving active opponents requires a large repertoire of different movements. The inclusion of simple basic movements in complex drills creates the necessary platform for a learning process that will allow players to use them at a later stage in competitive matches.

Small sided games

Games of 1 v 1, 2 v 2 or even between unevenly matched teams (e.g. 2 v 3) stimulate the players to use their dribbling and feinting skills. Youth coaches often exploit this in their training programs. Yet one thing is often forgotten.

How can a player in a small sided game participate fully when he has never learned the techniques needed in 1 v 1 situations?

In fact, only players with innate talent or with good powers of observation and imitation will be able to resist an opponent's determined challenge.

All other players will be hopelessly out of their depth, because they have not mastered the necessary skills such as feinting and the ability to run with the ball under close control. They often lack any sense of touch for the ball. An opponent only needs to wait for such a player to make an elementary mistake (e.g. to allow the ball to roll too far away from his foot) and can then seize the opportunity to step in and take the ball.

Under these circumstances, attackers will inevitably become frustrated and defenders will gain in confidence.

The situation is different when the players have learned a number of feints during previous training sessions. Small sided games are then an excellent setting for learning.

1 v 1 as a line game

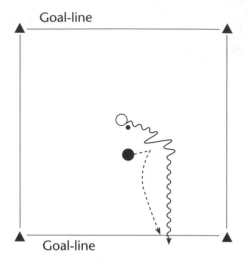

Rules of the game

Two players play 1 v 1 in a square measuring 10 x 10 yards. Each player must defend the whole width of the line behind him between the 2 cones. A goal is scored when the attacker dribbles past the defender and over the defender's goal line. The players then swap roles.

The playing time should not be too long (no more than 1 minute), otherwise the players will become fatigued. The game can be alternated with pauses, during which the players can practice their skills (e.g. juggling the ball).

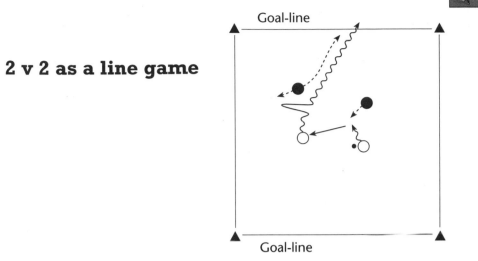

2 v 2 as a line game

Rules of the game
There are several variants of 2 v 2. Each player can either dribble the ball or pass to his partner. Nevertheless, many 1 v 1 situations arise, giving the attackers the chance to practice what they have learned.

Other games
1 v 2, 2 v 3, 3 v 3, 3 v 4

When a lone attacker takes the ball past 2 opponents outside the opposition's penalty area and goes on to score, the dribbling practice has been successful.

4 v 4 with 2 goals and 2 goalkeepers

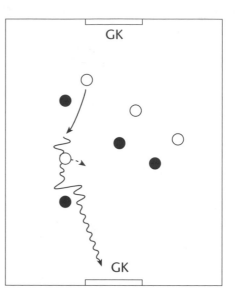

- Two junior goals are placed 20 yards apart.

Each team consists of a goalkeeper and 4 field players. In the small playing area the players have lots of opportunities to use the feints they have learned to enable them to get into shooting positions. In this game passes alternate with dribbles. The coach can manipulate the rules to change the nature of the game. For example, goals scored after a successful run or after a successful dribble or after a one-two might count double.

Using basic movements in game situations

Players should be given the chance to dribble successfully in proper games and not just in training sessions. They should therefore use their newly acquired basic movements not only in closed circuits such as the Zig-zag or the Figure-8, but should also be given an early opportunity to use them in real game situations.

The players should be able to understand from the very beginning why it is important to master these basic techniques until they can perform them automatically. After an intensive practice phase, a coach should always provide his players with opportunities to use their newly acquired techniques creatively. It is therefore worthwhile encouraging them to vary and combine these basic movements while going round the various circuits.

Combinations of feints can also be practiced in isolation, so that the player can learn which feints to use in sequence.

Sometimes a single feint is not enough to send an opponent the wrong way. The attacker should then be able to carry out a second feint to help him to dribble successfully past his opponent.

The following pages show a small selection of the possibilities.

Dribbler to side of opponent

Double change of direction

(a) The attacker makes a fast run with the ball to the base line, screening the ball from the defender, who runs alongside him.

(b) The attacker slows his run and prepares to change direction through 180 degrees.

(c) He plays the ball in the reverse direction with the inside of his left foot and transfers his weight to his right foot.

(d) He then leans back to the left, transferring his weight to his left foot, and changes direction by playing the ball towards the base line again with the inside of his right foot.

"Leo" trick

(a) The attacker makes a run with the ball towards the base line, screening the ball from the defender, who runs alongside him.

(b) He slows his run and feints to back-heel the ball.

(c) He draws his heel back over the top of the ball.

(d) He plays the ball forward again with his instep and accelerates to leave the defender behind.

Dribbler facing opponent

Matthews trick and scissor (outside-outside)

(a) With the ball at his feet, the attacker runs towards the cone or a defender, then taps the ball to his left with the inside of his right foot

(b) He prepares to carry out a scissor with the outside of the right foot.

(c) He carries out a scissor, swinging his right foot across the front of the ball from left to right.

(d) He puts his right foot to the ground, then plays the ball to the left with the outside of his left foot.

(e) He plays the ball forward with the inside of his left foot and sprints away from the cone (defender) with the ball at his feet.

85

Foot on the ball drag-back and drag behind standing leg

(a) The attacker feints to shoot with his right foot, with the purpose of making the defender take defensive action.

(b) The attacker stops the ball by putting his right foot on it.

(c) He drags the ball back under the sole of his right foot.

(d) He plays the ball to his right with the inside of his right foot, threatening to make a run in that direction.

(e) The defender follows alongside him.

(f) The attacker feints to shoot with his right foot, with the purpose of making the defender take defensive action.

(g) The attacker twists his right foot inward in front of the ball, and pulls the ball back with the front of this foot.

(h) He pulls the ball back behind his standing leg leaving the defender still moving in the other direction, then sprints away from the defender.

Dribbler with back to opponent

Scissor (inside-inside) and drag behind standing leg

(a) The attacker carries out a scissor by swinging his right foot from right to left across the front of the ball and then puts his right foot to the ground.

(b) He takes a pace with his left foot, then leans to the right, transferring his weight to his right foot.

(c) He carries out a scissor by swinging his left foot from left to right across the front of the ball.

(d) He puts his left foot to the ground.

(e) He turns to his left and plays the ball to his left with the inside of his right foot.

(f) He feints to shoot with his right foot.

(g) He suddenly twists his right foot inward and drags the ball back with the front of his foot.

(h) He drags the ball behind his standing leg and positions his body between the ball and the defender.

(i) He sprints away from the defender.

Scissor (inside-outside) and change of direction (inside)

(a) The attacker carries out a scissor (inside) with his right foot, puts his right foot to the ground, takes a pace with his left foot and transfers his weight to his left foot.

(b) He then carries out a scissor (outside) with his right foot.

(c) He puts his right foot to the ground, then transfers his weight to his left foot, screening the ball from the defender.

(d) He plays the ball to his left with the inside of his right foot, keeping his body between the ball and the defender.

(e) He sprints away from the defender with the ball at his feet.

Circuits

Drills for large groups

When I started to explain the subject matter of the "Schalke basic training" in courses and seminars a number of years ago, I also started to systematize the large number of organizational forms. Many of these, and the associated technical elements, were derived from the famous videos by Wiel Coerver.

One of these forms in particular attracted my attention, and I needed a lot of time before I fully understood it. Sixteen youngsters dribbled systematically in complex circuits after starting at four different points. It was a type of zig-zag circuit, in which the youngsters dribbled in specified paths.

At that time I called this a drill for large groups, because almost any number of players can participate. The larger the number, the more cones are used, thus ensuring that none of the players have to stand around waiting their turn.

This zig-zag offers only a limited number of options, however, because the angles are always the same.

There is no possibility of practicing a forward and backward movement or a 180-degree turn.

During a basic training session I had the idea of placing the cones in such a way that the players would have to carry out lots of turns through 180-degrees. I called this new circuit the "**Comb**," because it bears some resemblance to a comb. This circuit is especially suitable for practicing techniques such as the scissor (inside-inside) and the drag behind the standing leg. Today the comb is the favorite drill of many youngsters.

After experimenting with other circuit shapes, other angles and new continuous drills, I devised the **Christmas Tree**, the **Thunderbolt** and the **Figure-8**.

Features of the method

• Turning in front of the cone

The first instruction to the players is "Turn in front of the cone!"

This rule is especially important for drills involving a lot of players, e.g. the **4-fold Zig-zag** or the **4-fold Comb**, when there is a high risk of collisions occurring if it is not obeyed. It ensures that players can arrive at the cones simultaneously without causing chaos.

• Learn the circuit first

Each new drill with a large group makes considerable demands on the players' sense of orientation. Before they start to practice specific techniques, they must have a clear grasp of the route that they have to follow among the many cones that mark the circuit.

When the players are introduced to a new circuit, the first step is to walk or jog round the route while carrying a ball or even without a ball. This ensures that they can focus completely on the route.

The coach should avoid long explanations but should simply ask them to follow a player who knows the route or lead them round the circuit himself.

The next step is for the players to follow the route with a ball at their feet but without having to carry out any set movements.

The most skilled players will experiment and demonstrate various techniques to the coach.

Beginners will use simple techniques and are satisfied when they are able to follow the correct route. When the players are familiar with the circuit, the various techniques can be selectively practiced. Only then can the players be asked to carry out specific tasks, techniques and combinations of techniques, and practice how to use them creatively.

• Warming-up or core session?

The drills for large groups are just as valuable for warming-up as for the core part of a coaching session. During warming-up the players can carry out familiar movements at an easy tempo, while during the main session the coach can introduce new movements or ask the players to carry out familiar movements at speed.

If players need to repeat techniques or improve their execution, they simply set off on another circuit when they reach the starting cone.

The coach can call out the techniques that he wants them to use.

The players hear the coach's instructions and switch immediately to the required technique.

When new techniques are introduced, it is advisable to carry out one trial circuit first, during which the coach can call out instructions or corrections, before proceeding with a "proper" practice circuit.

- **The drills for large groups are suitable for:**
- Warming-up
- Learning basic movements until they become automatic: dribbling with left and right foot, changes of direction and rotations with the ball, special foot and leg movements, feints for a variety of game situations.
- Motivational running conditioning

Zig-zag

The Zig-zag enables important key movements to be practiced simply. It is the simplest of the drills for large groups.

Only a few cones are needed to organize a very effective dribbling session. The cones can be set up with a variety of angles and distances.

Basic Zig-zag:

a) Steep   b) Flat

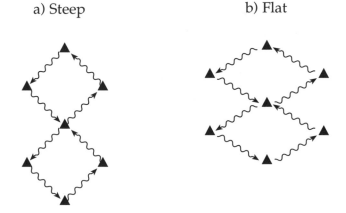

The type and difficulty of the techniques that can be practiced change depending on the chosen angles.

The coach should set the distances between cones to match the capabilities of the players and his coaching objective.

The younger the players, the shorter the distance needs to be. However, when a coach wants his players to carry out basic movements after a longer run-up at higher speed, then he simply increases the distance between the cones.

2-fold Zig-zag:

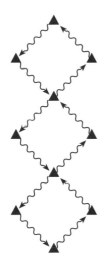

The 2-fold Zig-zag circuit has one starting point and one turning point.

Only seven cones are needed to set up a 2-fold Zig-zag circuit for up to 8 players.

The Zig-zag can be extended if required.

The distance between cones can be increased or decreased as required.

4-fold Zig-zag:

The 4-fold Zig-zag is the most important version. It has 2 starting points and 2 turning points.

Two players frequently arrive at a cone simultaneously. They are therefore forced to take their eyes from the ball to observe what is happening around them.

The players use both feet to run and turn with the ball.

94

6-fold Zig-zag

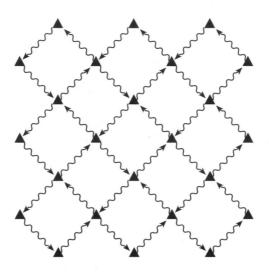

A 6-fold Zig-zag can accommodate a school class of 30 children without any difficulty. The different levels of skill of the children present no problems, because the teacher can assign the better players a more difficult task than the beginners.

Some players might be able to change direction fluently, while others might have mastered the rotation.

At soccer schools I have often demonstrated the Zig-zag with more than 120 youngsters. On an area stretching from the center line to the sideline and from one penalty area to the other, youngsters aged 8 to 14 have demonstrated numerous techniques on command. Parents could see that their children had learned a lot in just 3 days and that they were able to demonstrate their skills in a disciplined way in a very large group.

Procedure

The following procedure has proved successful in practice:

1. **Familiarization with the route, carrying the ball**
   The youngsters run round the new circuit to familiarize themselves
   with the route.
2. **Familiarization with the route, with the ball at the feet**
   In the second step the youngsters run round the circuit with the ball at
   their feet, using any techniques they wish.
3. **Change of direction (inside)**
   The simplest way to change direction in the Zig-zag is with the inside
   of the foot. This must be practiced with both feet. Beginners soon learn
   this technique.
4. **Change of direction (outside)**
   The next step is to learn the change of direction with the outside of the
   foot. This must also be practiced with both feet.
5. **Alternate change of direction (inside) and**
   change of direction (outside)
   The next step is the switch from inside to outside, using the same foot.
   The youngsters can start with their stronger foot, but must also
   practice with their weaker foot.
6. **Dummy step, step-over, scissor**
   When the youngsters have mastered the change of direction
   (outside) they soon learn how to use the dummy step.

The progression to the step-over and scissor is then relatively easy, because the only difference is in the leg movement.

The dummy step is performed by taking a sideward step with the leg behind the ball, the step-over is a sideward step over the top of the ball, and the scissor is a sideward step with the leg in front of the ball.

7. **Rotation (inside)**

   One of the most important basic movements is the rotation with the inside of the foot. The rotation is similar to a double change of direction. The difference is that the initial change of direction is made in the opposite direction to the direction that the player finally wants to take. When a player wants to turn left, he makes a rotation to his right, turning clockwise through three-quarters of a circle. When a player wants to turn right, he makes a rotation to his left, this time turning counterclockwise through three-quarters of a circle. A rotation (inside) can be preceded by a feint (see p. 42).

8. **Rotation (outside)**

   Skilled players like to rotate using the outside of the foot. Beginners usually find this difficult. A rotation (outside) can also be preceded by a feint (see p. 45).

9. **Foot on the ball trick**

   The Zig-zag is eminently suitable for practicing the foot on the ball trick until it can be performed automatically.

   The player drags the ball back with the sole of his foot and then sprints to the side toward the next cone with the ball at his feet. He can use his instep or the inside of his foot after the drag-back.

10. **Drag behind the standing leg**

    The most difficult basic technique practiced in the Zig-zag is the drag behind the standing leg.

    The player uses his left foot when he wants to turn right and vice versa. He drags the ball back and then flicks it behind his standing leg in the desired direction.

11. **Combinations of various techniques**

    When all of the techniques have been practiced, the coach can ask the players to carry out various combinations. For example, they could alternate between change of direction (inside) and rotation (inside). The change of direction must always be carried out with the same foot. Change of direction (inside) with the right foot, then rotation (inside) at the next cone with the left foot.

    Another option is a combination of the dummy step (outside-outside) and the foot on the ball trick.

    The youngsters can also be allowed to experiment with combinations of their own choosing.

The Christmas Tree

Creative dribblers can draw on a wide repertoire of feints and body swerves. Even while they are being coached in the basics, players should learn to carry out numerous movements in a variety of circumstances and practice them until they become automatic.

The Christmas Tree includes different angles and therefore provides new opportunities for carrying out turns and changes of direction with techniques that do not proceed in the same way as in the Zig-zag.

Basic Christmas Tree

The Christmas Tree, like the Zig-zag, provides a good framework for motivational dribbling coaching. It gives coaches the opportunity of selectively controlling their coaching sessions. All of the players are continuously in motion, have lots of ball contacts, and practice new movements systematically.

They therefore improve their touch and ball control skills very efficiently. A coach can use this second circuit to let his players practice basic movements in very varied ways. He has all of his players in his field of vision, so he can motivate and correct them, thus initiating learning processes selectively.

The coach arranges the cones as shown on p. 99. Only 6 cones are needed for the basic element, which is suitable for 4 to 6 players.

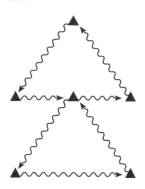

Basic Christmas Tree
(steep)

Basic Christmas Tree
(flat)

2-fold Christmas Tree

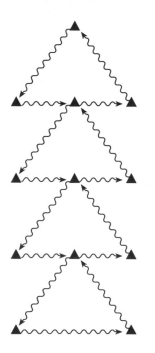

The basic Christmas Tree can be extended at will, so that the players have to run past more cones before they reach the turning point.

The base of the Christmas Tree is formed by 2 cones.

The next levels contain 3 cones.

At the tip is a single cone, which is the turning point.

The distance between the 2 cones forming the base is between 6 and 10 yards.

The distance between the cones should be chosen to suit the age of the players.

The older the players, the wider the distance.

The speed with which the players run with the ball should steadily increase.

Route

The players start at the bottom right cone and run diagonally towards the center cone of the next line, then towards the right-hand cone, then diagonally to the next center cone, etc. until they reach the turning point. Because the players have to learn to use both feet, they should sometimes start at the bottom-left cone.

The 2-fold Christmas Tree, which is suitable for up to 8 players, has one starting point and one turning point.

4-fold Christmas Tree

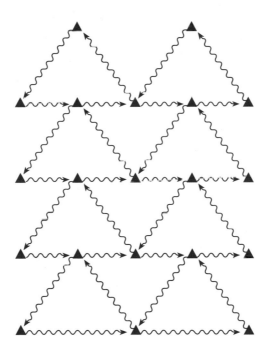

The 4-fold Christmas Tree is suitable for larger groups, such as a complete team. Its advantage is that the players frequently arrive simultaneously at the central cones. They have to lift their heads to look around and avoid getting into the path of the player who is approaching the cone from the other side.

The coach can ask the players to use the right or left foot, and turn to the right or the left.

Christmas Tree techniques

Simple change of direction

The change of direction toward the center, without making a rotation, can best be carried out with the following movements: change of direction (inside), change of direction (outside), dummy step/step-over/scissor (outside-outside) and (outside-inside).

The players carry out a dummy step at the outside cone

The players use the outside of the left foot to take the ball toward the center cone.

Rotation

Another option is to carry out a rotation (inside), The players soon learn to orientate themselves quickly after a rotation and to screen the ball from a defender, and they improve their ball control and touch.

The players run toward the outside cone with the ball at their feet.

They change direction (inside)

They perform another change of direction (inside).

The rotation (inside) can be preceded by a scissor towards the central cone.

Another option is a rotation (outside).

The movements listed below can be carried out at the outside and central cones.

The foot used to change the direction of the ball changes from cone to cone.

If a player carries out a rotation (inside) with his right foot at the first central cone, he must carry out a rotation (inside) with his left foot at the next outside cone.

Combinations of techniques

Outside cone
Change of direction (inside)
Change of direction (outside)
Rotation (inside)
Rotation (outside)
Dummy step
Step-over
Scissor
Drag behind standing leg
Foot on the ball trick

Central cone
Change of direction (inside)
Change of direction (outside)
Rotation (inside)
Rotation (outside)
Dummy step
Step-over
Scissor
Drag behind standing leg
Foot on the ball trick

Thunderbolt

To be able to practice dribbling past a frontal opponent, a route is needed that takes the player to the right or left after approaching an opponent (cone) from the front.

The Thunderbolt enables players to practice the Matthews trick or the scissor (outside-outside) in this situation.

At the outside cones the players can repeat the movements they practice in the Christmas Tree, while the central cone is suitable for movements involving a 90-degree change of direction.

The different circuits therefore complement each other while enabling the players to practice and improve already learned techniques.

By practicing different techniques in a variety of circuits, the players learn to use them flexibly.

Basic Thunderbolt

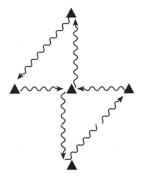

Basic Thunderbolt (steep)

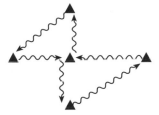

Basic Thunderbolt (flat)

The routes in the Thunderbolt are:
diagonal to the outside - across to the center - forward - diagonal to the side, etc.

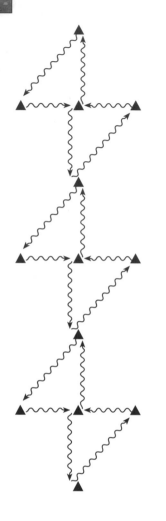

2-fold Thunderbolt

A Thunderbolt with one starting point and one turning point is termed a 2-fold Thunderbolt.

Eight players can practice simultaneously. After the first diagonal run to the outside cone, the same techniques are needed as for the Christmas Tree.

For example, a beginner might start with a change of direction (inside), while a more advanced player might carry out a rotation (inside).

All of the Zig-zag techniques can be used at the central cones (see combinations for Thunderbolt).

The key coaching aspect comes in the third leg of the circuit.

When the player runs frontally toward the cone, he can choose from a number of suitable techniques.

He could, for example, use the dummy step, step-over or scissor (outside-outside). The Matthews trick and the foot on the ball trick, preceded by a feint, are also very good options for dribbling the ball past the frontal cone.

At this point an opponent could be introduced to make the situation more realistic.

4-fold Thunderbolt

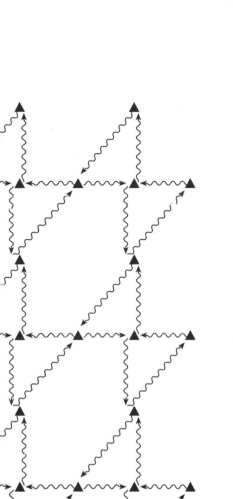

The 4-fold Thunderbolt has 2 starting points and 2 turning points and is suitable for a whole team. Depending on the number of players, the coach can set up 3 or 4 Thunderbolts in sequence. Players should not have to stand and wait at the starting point.

For very large numbers of players the coach can consider setting up a 6-fold Thunderbolt (not illustrated here).

Thunderbolt techniques

In this sequence the players demonstrate different techniques at different cones. While the player in the foreground carries out a rotation (inside) as he approaches the cone at the end of the first leg of the circuit, the player in the background carries out the Matthews trick as he approaches the cone at the end of the third leg. He does this by feinting to make a run to his left by tapping the ball to his left with the inside of his right foot, then playing the ball in a single fluid movement to his right with the outside of his right foot. He then sprints to the next cone, where he changes direction.

Player 1 dribbles toward the outside cone. Player 2 feints to run to his left.

Player 1 approaches the second cone. Player 2 taps the ball to his left with the inside of his right foot.

Player 1 has reached the second cone. Player 2 flicks the ball to his right with the outside of his right foot.

Player 1 starts a rotation (inside) by making a change of direction with the inside of his left foot. Player 2 sprints to his right toward the next cone.

Thunderbolt techniques

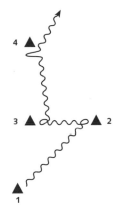

1. Starting cone
2. Outside cone
3. Central cone
4. Frontal cone

The techniques listed in the following table can be combined at will.
A coach should, however, only ask his players to combine 2 techniques
(e.g. change of direction (inside) - change of direction (inside) - Matthews
trick).

When the players have become familiar with the circuit they can try to
combine 3 different techniques (e.g. rotation (inside) - rotation (outside) -
scissor (outside-outside).

Combinations of techniques for the Thunderbolt

Outside cone	Central cone	Frontal cone
Change of direction (inside)	Change of direction (inside)	Feint to shoot + change of direction (inside)
Change of direction (outside)	Change of direction (outside)	Feint to shoot + change of direction (outside)
Rotation (inside)	Rotation (inside)	Matthews trick + scissor (inside)
Rotation (outside)	Rotation (outside)	Dummy step
Dummy step	Dummy step	Step-over
Step-over	Step-over	Scissor
Scissor	Scissor	
Foot on the ball trick	Foot on the ball trick	

The dummy step, step-over and scissor can be used with the inside or the
outside of the foot in all combinations (e.g. step-over (outside-outside) or
scissor (inside-outside).

Comb

The main coaching aspect of the Comb is the forward and backward movement. As many 180-degree changes of direction as possible are integrated into a fluid, continuous drill.

The players have to dribble in the following sequence of directions, which the coach should repeatedly call out during the first drills: forward - to the center - back - etc.

At the end of the first series, the players dribble the ball to the other side and start on their way back in the same sequence of directions:

forward - to the center - back - forward

Two different turns can be made (90 and 180 degrees):

- turn to the center: 90-degree turn
- at the central cone: 180-degree turn
- from the center in a forward direction: 90-degree turn

Basic Comb

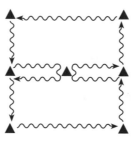

The basic Comb can be set up with 7 cones. It can accommodate 2 or 3 players.

The basic element can be extended at will so that the players have to run past more cones before they reach the turning point.

2-fold Comb

The 2-fold Comb with 16 cones can be used by 8 players simultaneously. The second player starts when the first player is on the second leg of the circuit, dribbling forward. If all of the players run at the same speed, they dribble in parallel to the center and back. The distance between the cones should be adjusted to suit the age of the players.

The dribbling speed should be gradually increased.

The most important instruction at the start of the drill is again, "Turn in front of the cone." The players should not dribble round the cone, otherwise there is a risk that collisions will occur with other players.

4-fold Comb

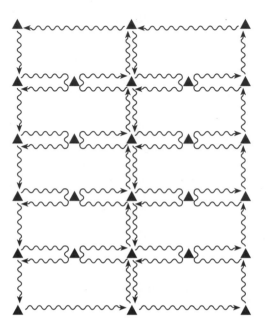

The most important type of Comb is the 4-fold Comb, which has 2 starting points and 2 turning points. Players arrive simultaneously at several cones within this circuit and are therefore forced to raise their heads and observe what is happening around them.

The players dribble and turn with both feet. The coach can call out the techniques that he wants them to use. The players hear his instructions and switch immediately to the required technique.

It is advisable to let the players carry out a trial circuit when a new technique is introduced. The coach can instruct and correct them during this circuit, then they can start on "proper" practice circuits.

Combinations of techniques

The following table shows a selection of techniques that can be practiced with the Comb.

90-degrees (1st cone)	180-degrees (center)	90-degrees (3rd cone)
Change of direction (inside)	Foot on the ball trick	Change of direction (inside)
Change of direction (outside)	Change of direction (inside)	Change of direction (outside)
Rotation (inside)	Change of direction (outside)	Rotation (inside)
Rotation (outside)	Scissor (inside-inside)	Rotation (outside)
Dummy step (outside-outside)	Drag behind standing leg	Dummy step (outside-outside)
Step-over (outside-outside)		Step-over (outside-outside)
Scissor (outside-outside)		Scissor (outside-outside)
Foot on the ball trick + inside of foot		Foot on the ball trick + inside of foot

Figure-8

Effective dribbling coaching requires numerous interesting circuits that repeatedly enable important basic movements to be practiced in similar, but for each player new, circumstances until they become automatic.
The final continuous drill in the section on coaching for large groups is the Figure-8.

New running and dribbling directions provide further opportunities to organize varied coaching sessions for dribbling.

This circuit also incorporates the typical principles that apply to coaching sessions for large groups:

- Use of both feet
- Frequent changes of direction
- Turns to right and left
- Changing angles
- Clearly understandable names for the techniques
- Lots of repetition

The Figure-8 circuit facilitates:

- Targeted learning
- Differentiation of performance
- Good motivation
- Room for creativity
- Meaningful, methodic buildup
- Immediate error correction

Basic Figure-8

The basic Figure-8 is a square in which the players dribble in the following directions: diagonally forward - back - diagonally forward.

Turns can be carried out to left or right. This changes the type and level of difficulty of the basic techniques at the cones.

For example, a player who completes the first diagonal run forward can then turn left by changing the direction of the ball with the inside of his right foot. This is a change of direction (inside). He could, however, make a clockwise rotation, guiding the ball with the inside of his left foot. This is a rotation (inside).

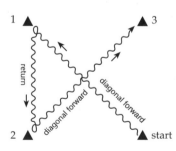

The players at the cone on the right dribble diagonally left to cone 1. They then carry out a change of direction or a rotation and dribble toward cone 2. They then dribble diagonally forward to cone 3.

This completes the first element.

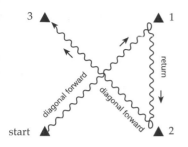

Players should practice with both feet. The Figure-8 should therefore also be carried out starting on the left side.

The dribbling directions are then: diagonally forward - back - diagonally forward.

Figure-8 - continuous drill

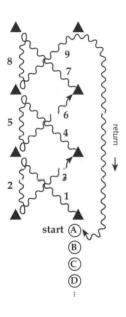

Figure-8 in only one direction
The basic Figure-8 can be used to create a continuous drill. Any number of squares can be arranged in sequence to create a typical drill for large groups. The players dribble in only one direction along the given route and then run round the outside to return to the starting point.

It is important that the players know exactly what route to follow, so that they can carry out their tasks "continuously" without difficulty. The coach has a good view of the whole circuit and can easily intervene to correct any errors.

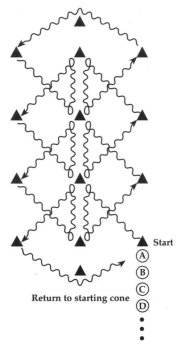

Turn to other side

Start

Ⓐ
Ⓑ
Ⓒ
Ⓓ
•
•
•

Return to starting cone

For more than 8 players, the coach should extend the row of squares to ensure that players do not have to queue at the starting cone.

The players can also dribble back down a second row of squares after going round a turning point.

This has two advantages:
• The coach does not need so many cones, because the central cones belong to 2 squares.
• The players meet at the central cones.
• The space is used efficiently.

Figure-8 techniques

The following techniques have proven effective, but have to be carried out differently. This depends on the direction of the turn and on which cone the player dribbles toward.

1. Change of direction (inside)
2. Change of direction (outside)
3. Rotation (inside)
4. Rotation (outside)
5. Foot on the ball trick + instep
6. Drag behind standing leg
    a) with the right foot
    b) with the left foot
7. Dummy step
8. Step-over
9. Scissor

The dummy step, step-over and scissor can be carried out with all combinations of the inside and outside of the foot.

Dummy step (outside-outside)

Dragging the ball back with the sole of the foot and playing it behind the standing leg

The player stops the ball by putting his foot on it and drags it back under the sole.

He then plays the ball behind the standing leg with the inside of his foot.

Drag behind the standing leg

In contrast to the drag back under the sole of the foot, the player uses the front of his foot to drag the ball behind his standing leg in one fluid movement, without stopping the ball.

With the left leg in front of the ball, twist the right foot inward.

With the front of the right foot or the right instep, drag the ball behind the standing leg.

Quickly turn left and head back to the next cone.

The drag behind the standing leg can be carried out with the right or the left foot.

The direction of the turn, the angle of the change of direction and the angle through which the player has to turn his body can therefore differ widely. The players experience these differences as new basic movements and should master both directions.

Combinations of different circuits

The circuits used for continuous drills in training sessions with large groups can also be combined. This results in a variety of angles within a single circuit and makes more demands on the youngsters' sense of orientation.

This chapter contains a number of examples, which are intended to stimulate creative coaches to develop their own combined circuits.

In principle a coach can give his imagination free rein in devising these circuits

The regular changes and the combinations of different drills prevent the players from becoming bored and force them to maintain their concentration. The stimulus of new circuits and the variable application of the techniques support the learning process.

Combination of Comb and Zig-zag

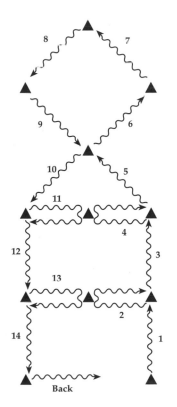

The diagram shows a combination of the Comb and the Zig-zag.

The players start with the typical techniques required for the Comb. In the course of the drill, they switch to the Zig-zag, which requires the techniques to be carried out differently.

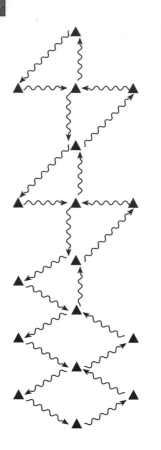

Combination of Zig-zag and Thunderbolt

Combination of Christmas Tree and Comb

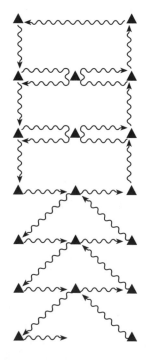

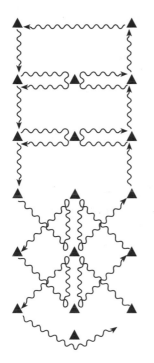

Combination of Figure-8 and Comb

Combination of Comb, Zig-zag and Thunderbolt

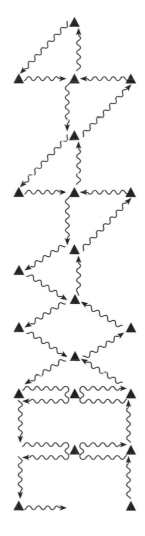

120

Link with follow-up actions

Continuous drills can also be linked with follow-up actions. The follow-up actions listed here can be integrated into drills for large groups:
- passes
- shots at goal
- coordination drills
- drills with a pendulum trainer

After a series of dribbling movements and feints in the Zig-zag circuit, the players run with the ball toward the coach or a teammate, pass the ball to him, receive it back, and then continue the Zig-zag circuit to the starting point. Follow-up actions can be carried out (same or different) at both sides.

Passes

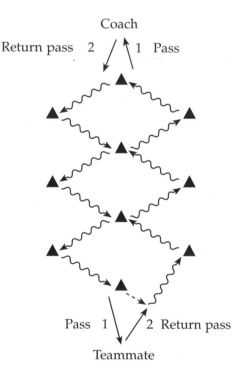

Coach

Return pass 2 1 Pass

Pass 1 2 Return pass

Teammate

Zig-zag drills and pass to teammate

The dribbler passes to his teammate with the inside of his foot and the teammate passes the ball back so that the dribbler can run onto it. The teammate could also pick up the ball and throw the ball back. The dribbler then has to control the ball before he can continue his run.

Shooting at goal

Youngsters are especially motivated by drills involving shots at goal. When the players have practiced the basic movements sufficiently, they can shoot at goal as part of a continuous drill.

As an additional task, the player might have to dribble past a defender before he shoots.

After shooting, the player dribbles back along the specified route and carries out another task on the other side of the circuit.

The continuous drill must not be long, otherwise the players will be exhausted when they come to shoot at goal.

The advantage of this circuit is that the players do not have to wait their turn to shoot, but are practicing basic movements.

Comb and shot at goal

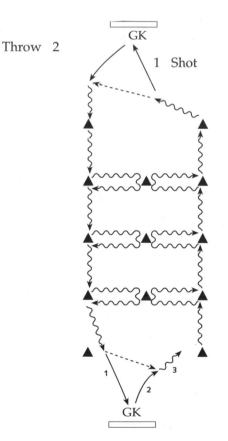

Coordination exercises

A dribbling drill can be combined with coordination exercises involving bars and tires.

When the players reach the marked zone, they leave the balls there, carry out a coordination exercise and then return to the dribbling drill.

As with shooting at goal, the players should not be overloaded. It is especially important that they are relaxed when they carry out coordination exercises. Functional gymnastics create the necessary recuperation pauses and serve to spread the load, i.e., to prevent it from becoming too one-sided.

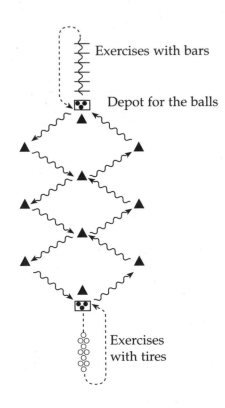

Exercises with bars

Depot for the balls

Exercises with tires

Pendulum Trainer

The Pendulum Trainer ia a training tool with 2 balls suspended from a "T". It can be adjusted easily and quickly, so heading and shooting exercises can be carried out in a child-friendly way.

After dribbling part of, for example, the Thunderbolt circuit, the player runs to the Pendulum Trainer and heads or kicks the ball. The ball cannot roll away because it is firmly attached. The players choose which ball to head or kick. There should not be any waiting time if 2 balls are available, but if there is, the distance between the players can be increased.

Dribbling circuit (Figure-8) and exercises with the Pendulum Trainer

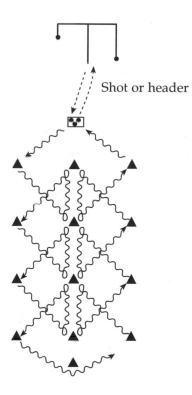

Shot or header

Training sessions for small groups

Most of the drills in this section are derived from videos of the "Coerver Method."

The drills for coaching small groups of 2, 3 or 4 players are organized according to the position of the defender.

The drill for the game situation "attacker sends defender the wrong way and dribbles past him" differs depending on whether the defender is in front of or behind the attacker or is challenging from the side.

The basic movements learned in the large-group sessions are used in the following drills.

Attacker facing defender

2 players

Player A starts at one cone and player B starts at the other. The 2 dribble toward each other and each carries out a previously agreed movement (e.g. dummy step (outside-inside) to the left) to avoid a collision. When they reach the cones they turn round and repeat the drill.

4 players

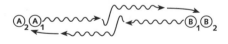

A1 and B1 dribble towards each other as in the drill above. A1 plays the ball to B2 and B1 plays the ball to A2. B2 and A2 control the ball and dribble towards each other.

Possible techniques

Dummy step, step-over, scissor, foot on the ball trick, Matthews trick, rotation (inside).

3 players and 1 ball

A dribbles round B and C, who are standing 4 and 8 yards away from his starting position.

B and C and then A move through one position (B to A, C to B and A to C).

A passes the ball to B, who then becomes the dribbler. Advanced players can pass the ball through the air.

B now dribbles round C and A after sending them the wrong way with a feint.

It is important for the players to know whether they are to take the ball past an opponent on the right or the left. They should, however, practice the basic movements to both sides.

The following movements are suitable for this drill:
- *Dummy step* (outside-outside)
- *Step-over* (outside-outside)
- *Scissor* (outside-outside)
- *Foot on the ball trick* + *inside of foot* (It is important to drag the ball back with the outside foot. If the attacker is to pass the defender on his (the attacker's) left, he should drag the ball back under the sole of his right foot.
- The following combinations of dummy step, step-over and scissor are possible: outside-inside; inside-outside.
- *Matthews trick*
- *Rotation (inside)*

3 players and 2 balls

The players stand in a line. Each outside player (A and C) has a ball. The player in the middle (B) is without a ball. A passes to B. B controls the ball and dribbles toward A, who runs toward him. B feints and dribbles past A, who then takes up position in the middle.

Player C then passes to A. A controls the ball and dribbles toward C, who runs toward him. A feints and dribbles past C.

The player in the middle thus always receives the ball from an outside player and dribbles past the outside player.

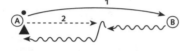

(1) A passes to B
(2) B controls the ball and dribbles toward A
(3) A runs toward B and B dribbles past A
(4) A takes up position in the middle

(1) C passes to A
(2) A controls the ball and dribbles toward C
(3) C runs toward A and A dribbles past C
(4) C takes up position in the middle

(1) B passes to C
(2) C controls the ball and dribbles toward B
(3) B runs toward C and C dribbles past B

In this way the players switch roles continuously.

Triangle with opponent
(drill for 6 players)

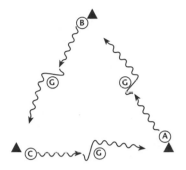

One attacker with a ball stands at each corner of the triangle. Each of the attackers starts to dribble towards the next corner. One defender is positioned at the middle of each side of the triangle. The attackers have to dribble past the defenders.

The attackers can dribble past the defenders on either side.

After a given time the players switch roles. The attackers go into the middle and the defenders become attackers.

The resistance offered by the defenders can be gradually increased.

Square with opponents
(drill for 8 players)

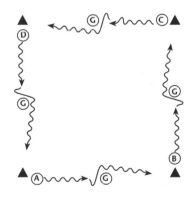

One attacker with a ball stands at each corner of the square. Each of the attackers starts to dribble towards the next corner. One defender is positioned at the middle of each side of the square. The attackers have to dribble past the defenders.

The attackers can dribble past the defenders on either side.

After a given time the players switch roles. The attackers go into the middle and the defenders become attackers. The resistance offered by the defenders can be gradually increased.

Triangle with center

One attacker with a ball stands at each corner of the triangle. The 3 players dribble simultaneously toward the cone in the center of the triangle. About one yard from the cone they feint (e.g. scissor (outside-outside) or Matthews trick) and dribble to the next corner cone.

The players wait until they have all reached their corner cone. At a pre-arranged signal or a start sign from the player in charge, they repeat the run to the middle and to the next corner, always proceeding around the corners in the clockwise direction.

After a given number of runs, the players switch to the counterclockwise direction to allow them to practice with the other foot.

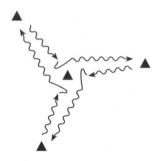
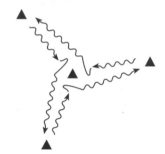

a) Clockwise   b) Counterclockwise

Square with center

The triangle with center drill can be carried out with a square instead of a triangle.

4 players then dribble simultaneously toward the cone in the center of the square, feint and dribble to the next corner cone.

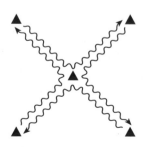
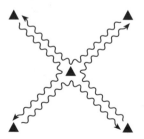

a) Clockwise   b) Counterclockwise

Attacker to side of defender

This section describes drills in which the players can repeatedly practice the basic movements that they need when an opponent challenges from the side.

There are 3 basic situations:

- The attacker tries to turn his back on the defender, drag the ball back and make a 180-degree turn to escape from the defender.
- The attacker turns inside, shielding the ball from the defender, and continues his run in another direction The following drills include turns through 90 and 60 degrees, so that the players can carry out a whole series of repetitions in a closed circuit.
- The attacker sends his opponent the wrong way, e.g. with a "Leo trick," (see page 91) and continues his run.

Drill for beginners

a) 4 to 8 players dribble towards a center cone. About 1 yard before they reach the cone, they turn and run back to their starting points. This necessitates a 180-degree turn.

Techniques that can be used
- Drag back under the sole of the foot
- Change of direction (inside)
- Change of direction (outside)
- Scissor (inside-inside)
- Drag behind the standing leg

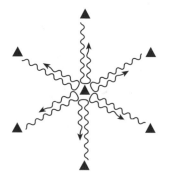

b) A player dribbles round the 3 sides of a triangle. There is no opponent. After 2 or 3 rounds he reverses his direction.

The following techniques are suitable for this drill:
- Change of direction (inside)
- Change of direction (outside)
- Rotation (inside)
- Rotation (outside)
- Foot on the ball trick - instep

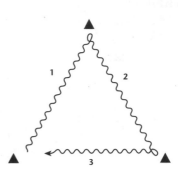

Continuous drill with opponent in triangle

A player dribbles around a triangle as in the basic drill described under a) above. An opponent running in the opposite direction challenges him.

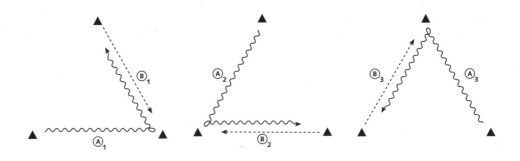

Challenge from the side (2 players)

The defender challenges from the attacker's right. The attacker then turns to the left through 180 degrees. The defender runs back and forth between the 2 cones so that the same practice situation always arises. After a given time or a given number of repetitions, the players swap roles.

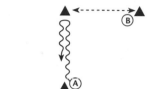

b) The defender now challenges from the attacker's left. The attacker therefore turns to the right through 180 degrees.

c) The defender no longer runs back to the starting cone but continues to the opposite cone. The attacker therefore has to turn right and left alternately. The defender must sprint convincingly toward the ball and simulate a challenge.

Continuous drill in square with opponent

In this drill there are 2 dribblers, who are challenged in sequence by a defender approaching from the front.

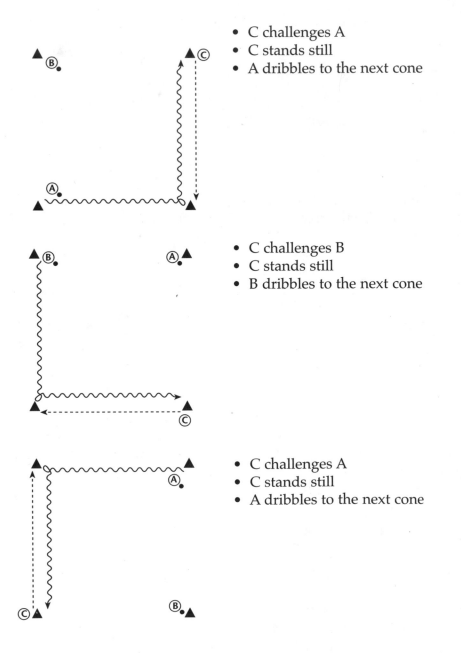

- C challenges A
- C stands still
- A dribbles to the next cone

- C challenges B
- C stands still
- B dribbles to the next cone

- C challenges A
- C stands still
- A dribbles to the next cone

Two dribblers -
one opponent on the diagonal

C runs along the diagonal and challenges A and B alternately.
A and B dribble to the center and "lose" the defender by carrying out a rotation (inside), then dribble to the next corner and back to the starting cone.

- C challenges A in the middle
- A carries out a rotation (inside) with his right foot
- A dribbles to C's starting point
- C runs to the diagonally opposite corner
- A dribbles back to his starting point

- C challenges B in the middle
- B carries out a rotation (inside) with his right foot
- B dribbles to C's starting point
- C runs to the diagonally opposite corner
- B dribbles back to his starting point

Attacker with back to opponent

The following drills are very suitable for practicing the basic movements for the "attacker with back to opponent" situation until they can be performed automatically (see pp. 67-77).

Preliminary drills between 2 cones

Preliminary drills between 2 cones

Individual practice

- Change of direction (inside) alternately with right and left
- Change of direction (outside) alternately with right and left
- Change of direction (inside) and change of direction (outside) alternately
    - with right
    - with left

Change of direction (outside)
between 2 cones

Change of direction (inside) and
- scissor/dummy step/step-over (inside-inside)
- scissor/dummy step/step-over (inside-outside)
- scissor/dummy step/step-over (outside-inside)
- scissor/dummy step/step-over (outside-outside)
- drag behind the standing leg

Change of direction (outside) and
- scissor/dummy step/step-over (inside-inside)
- scissor/dummy step/step-over (inside-outside)
- scissor/dummy step/step-over (outside-inside)
- scissor/dummy step/step-over (outside-outside)
- drag behind the standing leg

Same techniques on both sides

Scissor movements between 2 cones

- scissor/dummy step/step-over (inside-inside)
- scissor/dummy step/step-over (inside-outside)
- scissor/dummy step/step-over (outside-inside)
- scissor/dummy step/step-over (outside-outside)
- drag behind the standing leg

Combinations of techniques (examples)
- scissor (inside-inside) (right) + drag behind standing leg (left)
- step-over (inside-outside) (right) + dummy step (outside-inside) (left)
- drag behind the standing leg (right) + step-over (inside-outside) (left)

2-player drills

Scissor (inside-inside) at first cone with opponent

(a) When he is close to the cone, the attacker swings his right foot across the front of the ball.

(b) He puts his right foot to the ground.

(c) He braces himself with his left foot and starts to turn to his right.

(d) He plays the ball with the inside of his left foot, screening the ball with his body.

Directional dribbling

Directional dribbling can be used to allow groups of players to practice in series the foot and leg movements for the "attacker with back to opponent" situation.

After each feint (e.g. dummy step (outside-outside)), the players stop the ball, then they perform the same basic movement again, only faster. It is important that the basic movement is carried out with conviction. The coach can select the distance between the two turning points. The recommended distance is 6 to 12 yards.

Directional dribbling
Dribbling direction: right

When the series of basic movements in one direction is finished, the players should carry out the same sequence in the opposite direction. In this way they practice with both feet.

All of the techniques are now carried out in exactly the opposite direction.

A good tip for the players is: "When you want to dribble to the right, feint to the left. The first step is thus always in the opposite direction."

Directional dribbling
Dribbling direction: left

Basic movements - individual drills

Directional dribbling is very suitable for practicing the following basic movements until they become automatic:

1. **Dummy step**
   (outside-outside, outside-inside, inside-outside, inside-inside)
2. **Step-over**
   (outside-outside, outside-inside, inside-outside, inside-inside)
3. **Scissor**
   (outside-outside, outside-inside, inside-outside, inside-inside)

Directional dribbling. Playing the ball with the outside of the foot.

Directional dribbling with a shadow

All of the directional dribbling techniques can be practiced with another player. This gives the player a better "feel" for the real game situation. The second player shadows the attacker's movements, so that the attacker can sense the effect of his feints. After 2 runs the players can switch roles.

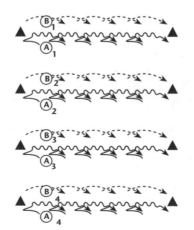

Game of "losing an opponent"

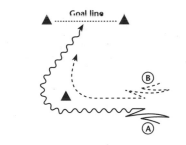

An attacker and a defender stand between 2 cones placed 4 to 6 yards apart. The attacker tries to "lose" his opponent by performing a rapid sequence of feints.

If the attacker succeeds in reaching the second cone on the right or the left, he scores 1 point. A skillful attacker can make his opponent lose his balance or can put him on the wrong foot, and he uses this small advantage to reach the second cone.

In another variant of this game, the attacker dribbles to the first cone and then over a goal line. He must try to continuously screen the ball. If the defender succeeds in kicking the ball away from the attacker's feet, the players swap roles.

Drills in a square

Individual drills

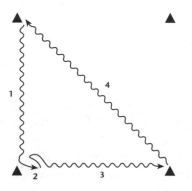

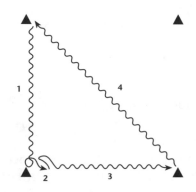

"Attacker with back to opponent" techniques in a square - turn to the left (toward the middle)

"Attacker with back to opponent" techniques in a square - turn to the right (away from the middle)

2-player drills (continuous task switching)

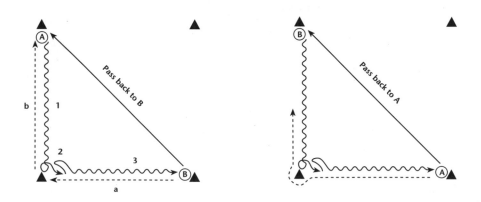

1. A dribbles to the cone in the middle, where B simulates a challenge
2. A rotates (inside) and "loses" B
3. A dribbles to the next cone and B runs to the dribbler's starting point.
4. A passes back to B

The drill is then carried out again, with B as the dribbler and A the defender.

4-man drills

One player stands at each corner of a square. A1 and A2 dribble toward B1 and B2, who remain beside their cones and serve as opponents.
After each dribble the players swap roles, because the players pass the ball to the nearest player in the counterclockwise direction.

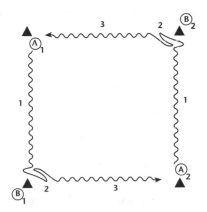

1. A1 and A2 dribble simultaneously toward B1 and B2.
2. They turn their backs to their opponents and carry out an "attacker with back to opponent" feint (e.g. dummy step (outside-outside)).
3. They dribble toward the next cone.

Phase 1

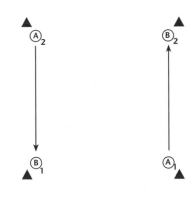

1. A1 plays the ball to B2.
2. A2 plays the ball to B1.
3. B1 and B2 control the ball and turn toward the next cone.
4. The dribblers look briefly at each other before they start.

Phase 2

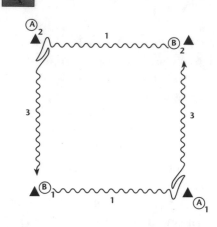

1. Now B1 and B2 dribble simultaneously toward A1 and A2.
2. They turn their backs to their opponents and feint (e.g. scissor (inside-outside)).
3. They dribble toward the next cone.
4. They then pass to the other players (as in phase 2).

Phase 3

1. B1 plays the ball to A2.
2. B2 plays the ball to A1.
3. A1 and A2 control the ball and turn toward the next cone.
4. The dribblers look briefly at each other before they start.

Phase 4

Continuous drills (Zig-zag or Comb)

The large-group continuous drills are eminently suitable for practicing typical basic movements for "attacker with back to opponent" situations. The Zig-zag and Comb are shown here as examples.

The players dribble toward a cone, turn their back to the cone, and carry out an "attacker with back to opponent" feint.

This can be used especially effectively with skilled players by combining techniques for "attacker facing defender," "defender challenging from the side" and "attacker with back to opponent."

Zig-zag

Comb

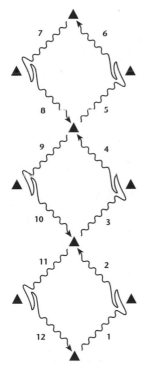

Drills for 3 players

The following drill closely resembles the real game situation "attacker with back to opponent."

The advantage of this drill is that the players switch roles. Each performs the tasks of the passer, the attacker and the defender in sequence.

This drill is also suitable for controlling and running with the ball in one fluid movement.

The drill: description and photos

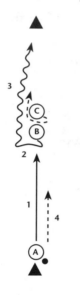

1. A (passer) passes to B (attacker).
2. B controls the ball, tricks C and dribbles past C.
3. B sprints away from C toward the next cone.
4. A sprints to challenge C and becomes his opponent.

(a) The attacker controls the pass with the inside of his right foot, taking it to his left.

(b) He feints to shoot with his right foot.

(c) Instead of shooting, he drags the ball behind his standing leg.

(d) He dribbles past the defender toward the next cone.

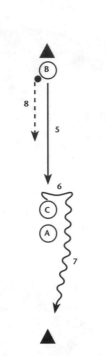

Now B is the passer, C is the attacker and A is the defender.

5. B passes to C.

6. C controls the ball and tricks A.

7. C dribbles toward the next cone.

8. B sprints to A and becomes the defender.

(e) The attacker turns round and becomes the passer.

(f) The defender (in white) becomes the attacker and sprints towards the ball.

(g) He controls the ball with the outside of his right foot without checking his run.

(h) He plays the ball to his right, away from the defender, with the outside of his right foot and dribbles to the starting cone. The drill then starts again.

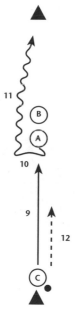

Now C is the passer, A is the attacker and B is the defender.

9. C passes to A.

10. A controls the ball and tricks B.

11. A dribbles toward the next cone.

12. C sprints to A.

In this way the drill can be continued with the players continuously switching tasks.

Drills with shot at goal

When the players have roughly mastered the basic drills, they should extend them with a follow-up action (see also p. 129).

This could, for example, be a shot at goal or a cross. This shows the players that the basic drills do have a purpose and establishes a link to real game situations.

Rotation and shot at goal

The players finish a series of basic movements (e.g. rotation (inside) or rotation (outside)) with a feint and a shot at goal.

This drill should also be carried out with the left foot.

The cones can also be replaced with passive or semi-passive defenders.

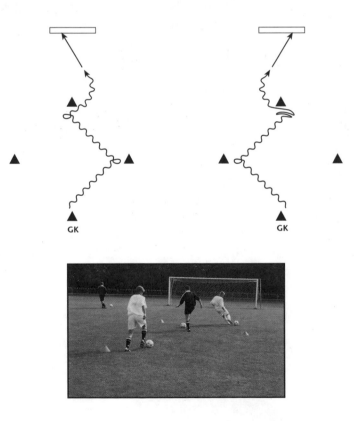

Pass, feint and shot at goal

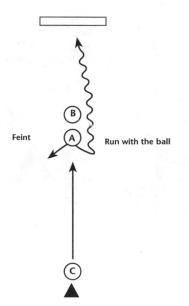

Feint   Run with the ball

The defender should initially serve only as an orientation point. He should thus only react to the feints. This allows the attacker to build up his confidence and improve his feinting technique. The better the attacker masters the techniques, the more resistance the defender should offer. When skilled players carry out this drill the defender genuinely tries to win the ball. In the first phase the attacker controls the ball before trying to trick the defender and dribble past him. He should use scissors, step-overs, dummy steps and the drag behind the standing leg as variably and creatively as possibly.

In the second phase the attacker should control the ball without checking his run, taking it past the defender and running toward goal. Just before the ball arrives he should put his opponent on the wrong foot by feinting to go in the other direction.

Beginners should decide the direction for themselves and the defender should react as required. The coach can take over the role of defender.

More advanced players should have mastered movements in both directions and should be able to trick the defender, who should genuinely try to win the ball. In this variant the players in the middle can regularly swap the attacker and defender roles.

A teammate or the coach can play the ball hard and low to the attacker.

Coaching Books from REEDSWAIN

#785:
Complete Books of
Soccer Restart Plays
by Mario Bonfanti and
Angelo Pereni
$14.95

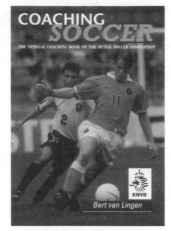

#154:
Coaching Soccer
by Bert van Lingen
$14.95

#177:
PRINCIPLES OF
Brazilian Soccer
by José Thadeu Goncalves
in cooperation with Prof. Julio Mazzei
$16.95

#185:
Conditioning
for Soccer
Dr. Raymond Verheijen
$19.95

#244:
Coaching the 4-4-2
by Maziali and Mora
$14.95

#765:
Attacking Schemes
and Training
Exercises
by Eugenio Fascetti and
Romedio Scaia
$14.95

Call REEDSWAIN 1-800-331-5191

Coaching Books from REEDSWAIN

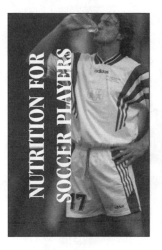

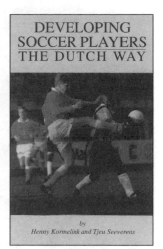
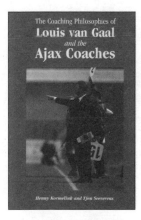
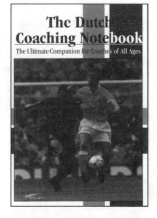

Coaching Books from REEDSWAIN

#291:
Soccer Fitness Training
by Enrico Arcelli
and Ferretto Ferretti
$12.95

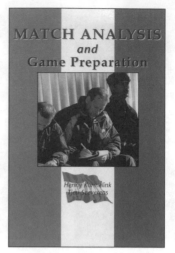

#261:
Match Analysis
and Game Preparation
Henny Kormelink and Tjeu Seevrens
$12.95

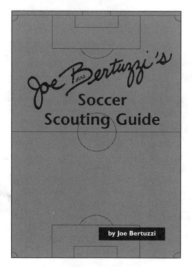

#789:
Soccer Scouting Guide
by Joe Bertuzzi
$12.95

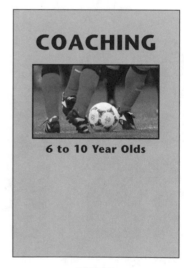

#264:
Coaching
6 to 10 Year Olds
by Giuliano Rusca
$14.95

1-800-331-5191 • www.reedswain.com